—African-American Biographies—

JESSE OWENS

Track and Field Legend

Series Consultant:
Dr. Russell L. Adams, Chairman
Department of Afro-American Studies, Howard University

Judith Pinkerton Josephson

 Enslow Publishers, Inc.

44 Fadem Road	PO Box 38
Box 699	Aldershot
Springfield, NJ 07081	Hants GU12 6BP
USA	UK

> For children everywhere, because Jesse Owens believed
> *". . . there's no such thing as an average kid."*

Library of Congress Cataloging-in-Publication Data

Josephson, Judith Pinkerton.
    Jesse Owens, track and field legend / Judith
Pinkerton Josephson.
        p.   cm. — (African-American biographies)
    Includes bibliographical references (p.) and index.
    Summary: Examines the life and accomplishments of Jesse
Owens, African-American Olympic gold medalist in track and
field.
    ISBN 0-89490-812-X
    1. Owens, Jesse, 1913-1980—Juvenile literature. 2. Track and
field athletes—United States—Biography—Juvenile
literature. [1. Owens, Jesse, 1913-1980. 2. Track and field athletes.
3. Afro-Americans—Biography.] I. Title. II. Series.
GV697.09J67 1997
796.42'092
[B]—DC21   97-17005
                                                                        CIP
                                                                         AC

Printed in the United States of America

10 9 8 7 6 5 4 3 2

Illustration Credits: Cleveland Public Library Photograph Collection,
pp. 36, 86; Cleveland State University, Cleveland Press Collection, pp.
29, 31, 34, 100; Courtesy of the Jesse Owens Foundation, p. 113;
National Archives, Still Picture Branch, p. 58; Ohio Historical Society
with the permission of the Ohio State University Athletic Department, p.
44; Ohio State University Libraries, Rare Books and Manuscripts, p. 24;
Ohio State University Photo Archives, pp. 6, 11, 40, 50, 54, 62, 66, 73,
76, 93, 105.

Cover Illustration: Ohio State University Photo Archives

Contents

Acknowledgments

For their encouragement and detailed critiques of the manuscript, thanks to Edith Fine, Karen Coombs, and my wonderful Encinitas writers' group. Thanks also to reviewers Russell L. Adams, James N. Giglio, and Hal Bateman, and to my editors, Damian Marie Shenko and Nina Rosenstein. I appreciate the help and insight provided by Marlene Owens Rankin, Ruth S. Owens, and Bud Greenspan. For research help and photo permissions granted, thanks to Rebecca Gray at the Ohio State University Photo Archives; the Ohio State University Libraries, Rare Books and Manuscripts; the Ohio State University Athletic Department; the Jesse Owens Foundation; Jean Collins at the Cleveland Public Library; the Ohio Historical Society; National Archives, Still Picture Branch; William Becker at Cleveland State University, Cleveland Press Collection; Illinois State Historical Library; Carrie Adam at the United States Olympic Committee Library; San Diego State University Library; Carlsbad Public Library, La Costa Branch, with special thanks to Pat Brunini.

Jesse Owens

1

A Hero in Berlin

M y life as a young man was almost all running . . . ," said Jesse Owens. "Each time I ran . . . I went faster."[1] In the summer of 1936, Owens and other athletes journeyed to Berlin, Germany. Germany's leader, Adolf Hitler, had spent money and time to prepare for the 1936 Summer Olympics. He had high hopes for the German athletes. Hitler wanted to prove that white people from northern Europe (Aryans) were better than those of other races. He did not count on a large group of African-American athletes from the United States track and field team stealing the spotlight. Leading that group was Jesse Owens, age twenty-three.

Owens had worked toward this moment for eight years. He had competed in track meets in junior high, high school, and college. Already, he had smashed records with a swift, fluid running style and a soaring long jump.

World events had almost canceled the games. In 1936, Europe was a bubbling cauldron about to boil over. Dictator Benito Mussolini had seized power in Italy. His armies had taken over the African nation of Ethiopia. Hitler and his army had marched into the Rhineland, west of the Rhine River. At Germany's borders, France and Belgium grew nervous. A civil war raged in Spain. As the Olympics drew near, many countries threatened to stay away. To prevent a boycott, Hitler put on his best behavior. He took down the anti-Semitic signs and billboards and welcomed the world to Berlin.

Ohio State's track coach, Larry Snyder, had come to Berlin with Owens. Before the American track and field athletes entered the stadium for their trial heats, Snyder warned Owens to expect a cold reception from the crowd. Hitler thought Jews, African Americans, Gypsies, and other groups were inferior human beings. The coach assumed that German fans might, too. Yet when Owens and the rest of the track team entered the stadium, the crowd cheered warmly. Germans already knew the name Jesse Owens.

Down on the track, German coaches and athletes swarmed around Jesse Owens. They jostled to talk to him. One coach studied Owens's sleek brown legs, as if trying to figure out the secret to his speed. The slender, five-foot-ten sprinter took the attention in stride. A modest, serious young man, Jesse Owens had a quiet charm and classy elegance that drew people to him.

The weather in Berlin had been stormy and wet during the week before the Olympics. Unlike today's quick-drying surfaces, tracks in 1936 were made from crushed cinders, which were pieces of partly burned coal. On August 3, the day of the 100-meter race, a noon cloudburst made the track surface messy and uneven. Runners knew that meant their leather shoes, heavy by today's standards, would soak up the moisture. The shoes would grow even heavier during the race.

Owens had drawn a starting post on the inside lane of a six-man field. He would have to run on the part of the track already churned up by other runners. Luckily, just before the race, the judges moved every runner over one lane. Now lane conditions would be roughly the same. Racing with Owens were Americans Ralph Metcalfe and Frank Wykoff, Erich Borchmeyer of Germany, Lennart Strandberg of Sweden, and Martinus Osendarp of Holland.

As Owens approached the track, he did not think about Hitler, the soggy track, or failing. He focused only on what he had to do on the field.[2]

"I was looking only at the finish line, and realizing that five of the world's fastest humans wanted to beat me to it," Owens said later. "There were six of us finalists, all with a gold medal ambition. Yet there could only be one winner. I thought of all the years of practice and competition, of all who had believed in me, and of my state and university."[3]

Like the other runners, Owens used a trowel to scoop out a starting place in the wet cinders. Owens dug in his toes. Every muscle poised, he hunched over. The fingers of both hands lightly touched the ground. At the crack of the starting gun, all six runners sprang cleanly forward.

Within ten meters, Owens pulled out in front with a smooth, effortless stride. His muscular legs churned. His feet barely touched the ground as he bounded across the finish line. Fellow African-American Ralph Metcalfe came in second, a yard and one-tenth of a second behind. Martinus Osendarp of Holland placed third. Owens had tied both the world and Olympic record time of 10.3 seconds. The spectators went wild, their cheers erupting into a roar.

Proudly, Owens stood on the victory stand to receive his gold medal. He said later, "My eyes blurred as I heard 'The Star-Spangled Banner' played, first

Jesse Owens set a new Olympic record in the long jump with a powerful leap of 8.06 meters (26 feet 5½ inches).

faintly and then loudly, and then saw the American flag slowly raised for my victory."[4]

Winning his first gold medal was one of the happiest moments of Jesse's life.[5] He went on to win three more gold medals in the 1936 games, for the 200-meter race, the broad jump (now called the long jump), and as part of the 400-meter relay team.

German athletes dominated most other Olympic events. But in track and field, Jesse Owens and his teammates dashed Hitler's plans for a show of German power. The American men's track and field team had outscored, outjumped, and outrun most of the German athletes.

Jesse Owens returned to the United States a hero. Autograph seekers hounded him. Newspaper headlines, movie theater newsreels, and radio announcers praised him. Cheering crowds welcomed him home with parades in Cleveland, Columbus, and New York City. Winning four Olympic gold medals made him one of the most famous athletes in sports history.

2

EMMA OWENS'S GIFT CHILD

 ive-year-old Jesse Owens awoke, hacking and gasping for breath. In the dim light of dawn, Jesse could see his mother tending two huge kettles of boiling water hanging over the fireplace. Jesse moaned; he felt hot. Gently, his mother told him she had to take the bump off his chest. The family was too poor to take Jesse to a doctor. Jesse had had these mysterious growths before (probably boils, infected places on the skin). This time, she said, the bump on his chest was too close to his heart and lungs. Exhausted from coughing, Jesse only half listened to what his mother was saying. He watched her hold the blade of the kitchen knife in the fire.

Slowly she walked toward him with the knife. Fear trickled down the back of Jesse's neck.[1] Once, he had stepped into a steel trap meant for a wild animal. Would this hurt worse than that? Deep worry lines creased his mother's weary face. When she cut into the boil, Jesse screamed so loudly he thought it was some-one else. The sharp pain cut deeper and deeper. He saw tears stream down his daddy's face. Then Jesse dropped into unconsciousness.

When he came to, the house was still dark. Was it nighttime now? he wondered. His older sisters and brothers were all sitting around the small, run-down shack they called home. Sharp pain raked across his chest like a bear's claw. He felt wet, as if someone had sprayed him with water. Except the wetness was his own blood.

Kneeling by Jesse's bed, his mother prayed con-stantly. Every few minutes she opened her eyes and mopped up the blood seeping from Jesse's wound.

Finally she slumped against the bed, dozing. Somehow Jesse got out of bed and dragged himself across the floor toward the front door. On the porch in the darkness of a moonless Alabama night, his father knelt in prayer.

"He's my last boy—J.C.'s the one you gave me last to carry my name," Jesse heard his father say. ". . . She always said he was born special—she said he was made when he couldn't be—"[2] Jesse's father told God that if little Jesse died, his mother would die, too. Then they would all die.

Hearing Jesse, Henry Owens turned, scooped the boy up in his arms, and told him to pray. Jesse did not remember what he said to God. But soon, the bleeding stopped. Jesse always believed that the power of prayer saved his life.

◆ ◆ ◆ ◆

James Cleveland Owens was born September 12, 1913, in Oakville, Alabama. The small, dusty community where he lived was little more than a cluster of small farms. The eighth of nine children, Jesse came along as a surprise to his parents after three boys and four girls. Jesse's mother called him her "gift child."[3] His father nicknamed him "J.C." Another baby, a girl, was born soon after Jesse. (One of Jesse's older sisters died as a young adult.)

Probably because of the cold, drafty house and his poor diet, Jesse suffered from chest colds and pneumonia, a serious lung disease. His family called the sickness a "powerful bad fever."[4]

Jesse's father, Henry Cleveland Owens, had been born to former slaves in 1878. Six feet two inches tall with powerful legs, Henry Owens always outran other men at neighborhood races on Sunday afternoons. Quiet but firm, he ruled his family with cautious wisdom. He believed that reading anything but the Bible would bring disaster to his loved ones. Worried about crop failures and seeing his family go hungry, he did not believe in store credit, and bought nothing that he could not pay for. Henry farmed the land as a sharecropper for white landowners. For this, he received a fifty-fifty split of crop earnings. To Henry, the worst thing you could do was make the "man on the hill" (the landowner) angry.

Jesse's mother, Emma Fitzgerald Owens, was a small, feisty woman with a lovely face and a kind voice. Much bolder than her husband, she believed that hopes and dreams were important. Like Jesse, she chose to see a silver lining within every dark cloud. She made her sons and daughters memorize a different Bible verse every week.

Feeding a family of growing children was not easy for Jesse's parents. Each fall, they butchered a hog or a cow and cured the meat in a smokehouse. That meat was saved for birthdays, holidays, and other special days. Most of the time, the family ate vegetables from the family garden, fruit from nearby orchards, and lots of soup. Jesse remembered, "Not starving was the best you could do."[5] Sometimes Jesse hid from neighborhood girls when he did not have enough clothes to cover his body.

On Sundays, the Owens family went to church with other African Americans. Young Jesse, dressed in pants and his one good shirt, sang hymns with the rest of the Baptist congregation. People clapped and swayed with the music. They listened, spellbound, as ministers preached soul-stirring sermons.

Like other children from sharecropping families, Jesse and his brothers and sisters hoed corn, picked cotton, and cut sorghum cane, which was used for molasses. By age seven or eight, Jesse could pick one hundred pounds of cotton a day. Though he could hardly see over the plow handle, he drove a mule to "bust the furrows," or bring up the soil around the cornstalks.[6]

On days when children were not in the fields, they went to school. In Alabama, as in much of the South, black children and white children received a separate, unequal education. In schools for white children, basic subjects were taught by trained teachers. Black children often went to school in the same ramshackle building that served as a church on weekends. Their teacher was usually a volunteer, not a trained professional. Rural schools closed during harvest or planting seasons. During his early school years, Jesse barely learned to read and write.

Even so, he came home one day talking about a special school, called a "kolledge [college]," where a person could learn how to be anything in the world. Jesse said he wanted to go there someday. His father wondered where Jesse had gotten such a crazy idea. But Jesse's mother hugged him and said that if he worked hard, maybe someday he *could* go to "kolledge."[7]

In Oakville, white families outnumbered black families. Except for the landowners, most white residents were sharecroppers, just like the Owens family. They, too, had little or no money or social status. The only difference was the color of their skin. Some of the Owenses' white neighbors looked down on black people. Jesse's way around ugly situations was to flash a sunny smile and extend his hand. This usually worked, though just like other kids, he still got into scrapes and fights.

In spite of the hardships, Jesse had a happy childhood. He and his older brothers went swimming and fishing. Sometimes they hunted possum or rabbit, camping out all night with their dogs. Jesse was too young to play on the local baseball team with his older brothers. Instead, he and his friends played tag, keep-away, and hide-and-seek. An older cousin recalled Jesse in those games: "He'd run and play like everybody else, but you never could catch him."[8]

"I always loved running," Jesse said. "It was something you could do all by yourself, all under your own power. You could go in any direction, fast or slow . . . fighting the wind . . . seeking out new sights just on the strength of your feet and the courage of your lungs."[9]

The year Jesse turned nine, a gnawing insect pest called the boll weevil invaded cotton fields. Whole crops withered and died. Since sharecroppers used their earnings to buy supplies, this meant less food on the table for the Owens family.

Racial tensions in Alabama and the rest of the South had also been building. The Ku Klux Klan (KKK), a secret group of white supremacists, terrorized blacks with random lynchings (illegal hangings and other killings). As a scare tactic, the Klan burned crosses on the front lawns of African Americans. Blacks were often arrested and charged with crimes on little or no evidence. Even so, Henry and Emma Owens did not teach their children to hate those who did this. During this period, over half a million African Americans in the South moved north. They carried with them hopes for a brighter future.

On a bleak Christmas Day in 1922, no Christmas tree or presents brightened the Owens household. That afternoon, Jesse asked his brother Sylvester where their parents were. Sylvester did not know. Neither did his little sister Pearline. Jesse took off through the fields. He finally spotted his parents in a corner of the family's forty-acre parcel. Even from a distance, Jesse could tell that they were arguing. He ducked down behind some boulders to listen.

Jesse heard the word "moving." He knew his sister Lillie now lived in Cleveland, Ohio, where she had married and found a job. Now she wanted her family to come to Cleveland, too. Jesse's mother said that the only way the children would survive was if the family moved north. Schools were supposed to be better there. If their children stayed in Oakville, they might never learn to read and write. They would have to sign their names with an *X*, just like their father.

Jesse's father asked what kind of a job he could possibly get in Cleveland. All he knew was farming. He told Emma the family would starve there. They were starving now, Emma reminded Henry. Then his father told his mother she was talking crazy, just like "J.C."

Jesse did not wait to hear what his parents decided. He raced back to the house, his mind already buzzing with thoughts of a new place to live, a new school, maybe even "kolledge." When his parents got back to the house, his mother announced that the family was indeed moving north. Everybody flew into action. Jesse's father and older brothers began packing and getting ready to return the farm tools and sell the farm animals to the landowner. The money would pay for the train tickets. Emma and her daughters began scrubbing down the house for the next tenants.

Jesse had a million questions for his mother. Where would they live? What would it be like? Where would the train take them?

"It's gonna take us to a better life," Emma Owens answered.[10]

Excited, Jesse rushed around the house helping with the packing. In his haste, he bumped into his father. Briefly, his father steadied himself by placing his hands on Jesse's shoulders. Henry Owens's hands were shaking.

3

JESSE FINDS
A MENTOR

 eaving Oakville, Alabama, and moving north was one of the hardest things Henry Cleveland Owens had ever done. Compared to tiny, quiet Oakville, with its some twelve hundred residents, Cleveland in 1922 was a loud, bustling city of about eight hundred thousand people. Back in Oakville, farm smells of soil, plants, and animals mingled under a clear blue sky. In Cleveland, fumes from factories, steel mills, and oil refineries clogged the air. The city fronted on Lake Erie, larger than any pond in Oakville. Cleveland also had more snow and ice than Jesse and his brothers and sisters had ever seen in their lives. On his first day up north, Jesse slipped on the ice and was almost run over by a car. His father scolded him about cars and big city streets.[1]

Many of Cleveland's white residents did not welcome the huge numbers of newly arrived black families. Often restaurants, theaters, and recreational buildings were "for whites only." Fearful of strangers, for the first six months Emma Owens kept the shades drawn.

The Owens family settled into an apartment in an east Cleveland ghetto. Other African-American families had moved there, as well as many recent immigrants from other countries. The apartment had running water and electric lights, exciting new luxuries for the Owens family.

Most of the Owenses' closest neighbors were Polish. Jesse's new friends did not mind his brown skin, and he did not mind their broken English. The neighborhood kids played stickball (a street form of baseball), tiddlywinks, and marbles. They went to movies and built a clubhouse. Sometimes the children stole apples from the corner grocery.

Everybody in the Owens family worked. Jesse's mother and older sisters cleaned houses and took in laundry. Henry and his older sons worked in a steel mill, unloaded freight cars, and worked as part-time janitors. Jesse delivered groceries and worked in a shoe repair shop, where he swept floors, washed windows, and shined shoes. Even though wages were low, the family could now eat meat once a week. And soon, Jesse had new shoes and clothes.

Jesse began school at racially mixed Bolton Elementary School. Even though he was nine and could read some, the principal put Jesse in the first grade. On the first day of school, his new teacher asked his name. In his southern drawl, he said "J.C." The teacher heard "Jesse." The name stuck.

A head taller than the other first graders, Jesse barely fit into his seat. He was later moved to a higher grade. From then on, he was always a few years older than his classmates. School was not easy for Jesse, partly because he had learned very little in Alabama. He also still suffered from bouts of pneumonia, made worse by the harsh northern winters.

In a few years, Jesse, fourteen, moved on to Fairmount Junior High School. He became president of the student council, captain of the hall guards, and captain of the basketball team.

At Fairmount, Jesse met Minnie Ruth Solomon, thirteen, a pretty, popular girl whose family was also from Alabama. Jesse liked the neat, stylish way Ruth dressed. The two passed notes back and forth, giggled, and flirted. Jesse carried her books from school. On their first date, they went to a movie and out for a soda. He said later, "I fell in love with her some the first time we ever talked, and a little bit more every time after that . . ."[2]

He also became close friends with Dave Albritton, another classmate from Alabama. Tall and lanky, Albritton called Owens "Shorty."[3] Both boys were interested in girls, food, and sports, especially the track team. The coach of that team, Charles Riley, would change Jesse's life.

Junior high track coach Charles Riley worked closely with Jesse Owens. "I grew to admire and respect his words and his actions . . . ," said Owens. "I wanted to be very much like him because he was a very wonderful person."

A short, wiry man with graying hair and glasses, Riley spoke with an Irish brogue and had a lively sense of humor. About the same age as Jesse's father, he was a well-liked teacher and coach. Jesse remembered Coach Riley as the "balance wheel."[4] Riley helped Jesse stay focused both on and off the track. The coach expected his athletes to show leadership and discipline in the classroom and sportsmanship on the field.

Spotting special qualities in the skinny teenager, Coach Riley started giving Jesse extra help. Riley suggested that Jesse run and do exercises each day after school. Jesse said his family counted on the money he earned from his after-school job. So Riley met Jesse for an hour-long practice session before school. Sometimes the coach brought Jesse breakfast.

To help Jesse learn how to keep his stomach in, his chest out, and his head forward, Riley attached a rubber sling to the gym wall. Jesse slipped into it like a harness. Then he ran in place, straining against the sling. His form improved, and his legs grew stronger.

On many Sunday afternoons, Riley drove his Model T Ford over to pick up Jesse. During lunches at Riley's home, he corrected Jesse's manners and talked with him about values, hopes, and dreams. Jesse learned skills that would help him grow as a man, as well as an athlete.

Coach Riley did not talk a lot about winning. Instead, he used little sayings to make a point, such as,

"You're training for four years from next Friday, Jesse."[5] By this, Coach Riley meant: Plan for the future, Jesse.

"Not a day passed that he didn't teach me something about running," Owens said.[6] For his part, Riley sensed that Owens was bright, quick, and eager to learn.

After watching Jesse tense up during races, Coach Riley took Jesse to watch horses race. He told him to stand by the rail and watch the better horses—for the looks on their faces and how their bodies moved. The horses' hooves raised clods of dirt as the animals thundered past, breathing hard. Their legs moved like the well-oiled gears of a machine. Jesse craned his neck to look at the horses' heads. Their faces stayed smooth.

On the way home, Riley asked Jesse what he had learned. Jesse said the horses made running look easy. Riley told Jesse that was because the horses' willpower and spirit were on the inside, not the outside. Jesse never forgot Riley's words.[7]

Riley had been training Jesse Owens for about a year when he ran the 100-yard dash in 11 seconds and the 220-yard dash in 27 seconds. Those were fast times for any runner. Riley had taught Owens to run lightly, as if the ground were covered with hot coals.

"The one big muscle in each thigh must do the lifting—quickly, cleanly and in a twinkling," said Riley.[8]

He told Jesse to blink his eyes when he ran, to relax his face.

In 1928, when Jesse was fifteen, he set new records for junior high school athletes in the high jump and the long jump. That same year, Owens met famous track star Charley Paddock. He had been a gold medalist in the 100-meter dash in the 1920 Olympics. (Many races in the United States were measured in yards. Internationally, the meter, which is longer than a yard, was used. A 100-meter race was nine yards and one inch longer than a 100-yard race.) People called Paddock "the world's fastest human."[9] He became Jesse's idol.

Under Coach Riley's kind, careful guidance, Jesse's life slowly started to become a race.[10]

4

AWAY WITH THE RUSH OF AN AIRPLANE

n October 1929, prices of stocks sold on Wall Street plunged. The country crashed into the Great Depression. Banks failed. People lost their jobs. Companies collapsed. Many people lost all their money. Cleveland, like other cities, did not have enough jobs to go around. Many African Americans had no way to make a living.

About this same time, Jesse Owens's father accidentally stepped into the path of a speeding taxi and broke his leg. The leg never healed properly. When Henry tried to return to work, he failed the physical for the steel mills. Before, eager for workers, company doctors had overlooked the defective left eye that Henry had always had. Jobs were now too scarce to allow for disabilities like poor vision. Henry Owens never worked steadily again.

By 1930, Jesse's older brothers had dropped out of school to work. A few got married and brought their wives home to live in the house the family rented. Emma and her older daughters continued to clean houses and take in laundry. Jesse's younger sister, Pearline, stayed in school.

During the Depression era, as many as twelve members of the Owens family lived in half of this duplex at 2178 East 100th Street in Cleveland. Pictured are Jesse's two sisters, his nieces, his mother, and his brother.

"We didn't starve," Jesse said later, "though hunger was something you lived with, like you lived with the color of your skin."[1]

After junior high, Owens moved on to East Technical High School in the fall of 1930. Like many other African-American athletes, he took vocational training classes to learn a trade. He did well in ceramics and other practical subjects, like shop. Even though he liked history, too, Jesse had never learned to read well, or how to study. However, he was levelheaded, hardworking, and good at discussing what he knew.

Owens had status because he was an athlete. Girls buzzed around him, charmed by his warm smile and neat appearance. But Jesse's heart belonged to Ruth Solomon.

The high school track coach asked Jesse's junior high coach, Charles Riley, to help out with the team. Riley was happy to continue working with Jesse Owens and other former students. Jesse's friend Dave Albritton was a star in the high and low hurdles and the high jump.

During one of Jesse's first high school races, he learned what it takes to win. As the runners took their positions at the starting line, every nerve in his body tingled. When the starting gun sounded, Jesse burst forward, rapidly taking the lead. He rounded the first curve of the track, then the second. He knew he-should probably save energy for the final stretch. Instead, he ran faster.

As Jesse moved into the home stretch, he heard the sound of steel spikes hitting the track behind him. The other runners were gaining on him. An inner voice screamed at Jesse not to let them pass him. With every last ounce of strength, he pushed forward.

Streaking across the finish line, Jesse felt the ribbon brush lightly across his chest. It was slack and loose— someone else had finished first. Jesse kept on running. He did not stop until he came to the schoolyard wall.

At East High, Owens became part of a powerful relay team that included Alfred Storey (seated), Jerry Williams (crouching), and his friend Dave Albritton (standing, left). Here, Coach Ed Weil (right) talks to his athletes.

Coach Charles Riley ran up to Owens and congratulated him. Puzzled, Jesse stared blankly at him.[2] The coach never made fun of his athletes. Then Riley told Jesse that even though he had not won, he had done something more important. Over and over, Jesse had beaten himself. Riley told Jesse that if he kept running that way, he might go all the way to the Olympics.

Encouraged, Jesse Owens worked to run faster and jump farther. Pretty soon, he began to cross the finish line first and feel the taut ribbon against his chest.

The summer after his junior year, Jesse went to Northwestern University in Illinois for track and field trials for the 1932 Olympics. He hoped to earn a spot on the Olympic team. For the first time, large numbers of black athletes were competing in a sport where white athletes excelled. Jesse lost to older, more seasoned athletes in the long jump and the 100-meter and 200-meter sprints. One runner who beat him was Ralph Metcalfe, a brilliant Marquette College student, much larger and stronger than Owens. Later that summer, Metcalfe and fellow African-Americans Eddie Tolan, Edward Gordon, and Cornelius Johnson won places on the United States track and field team.

Mirroring this changing scene in some sports, the entertainment field, too, was welcoming more African Americans. Musicians like big-band leader Duke Ellington, jazzman Louis "Satchmo" Armstrong, pianist Fats Waller, and singer Bessie Smith were starting to make jazz and blues famous.

Another milestone in Owens's life came when he was eighteen. Ruth Solomon gave birth on August 8, 1932, to their daughter Gloria. Owens later said that he and Ruth had secretly married some months before. Jesse's friend Dave Albritton had borrowed a car and acted as their best man and witness. After a wedding dinner of hot dogs and root beer, Ruth and Jesse had returned to their separate homes. They told no one else about their marriage. Both probably feared that their parents would think they were too young. When Ruth's parents found out, her father was furious and had the marriage annulled. Ruth dropped out of high school to work in a beauty parlor. Her parents helped take care of the baby. Ruth's father eventually forgave Jesse, so at least he could visit Ruth and the baby.

In the fall of his senior year, 1932, students at East High elected Jesse student council president. That spring, he became captain of the track team and finished first in seventy-five of the seventy-nine races he ran. In May, he broke the state long jump record by leaping 24 feet 3¾ inches (7.41 meters).

In mid-June 1933, Jesse competed at the National Interscholastic Championship meet at Soldier Field in Chicago. Again he sailed through the air with a leap of 24 feet 9⅝ inches (7.55 meters) to win the long jump. He ran the 220-yard dash in 20.7 seconds. Both scores

With Coach Riley's help, Jesse Owens soon learned how to burst across the finish line first. People began to call East Tech's track star the greatest high school runner of all time.

set new national records for high school boys. In the 100-yard dash, he tied the high school world record with a time of 9.4 seconds. Jesse's high school won the meet, with Jesse winning over half the team's total points. Dave Albritton won first in the high jump.

Back home, Cleveland threw its hometown speed king a victory parade. Jesse, his family, friends, and Coach Riley rode in cars through the downtown streets. Thousands cheered, including city councilmen and the mayor.

By now, the spotlight was firmly fixed on Jesse Owens. Sportswriters called the young track star "East High's one-man track and field show." They said he might become the "world's fastest human" (just like his idol Charley Paddock).[3] One reporter wrote, "Owens was away with the rush of an airplane but the grace of a fawn . . ."[4] Another called Owens the "Cinder Express" and said, "Owens is an unusual young man. . . . he prays at night that he won't become swell-headed [conceited]."[5]

No one was prouder of Jesse than his parents. Emma Owens's hair was graying now, and her face more wrinkled, but she still bubbled with optimism and pride for her son. Jesse knew his father, Henry Owens, was proud by the "smile that played around his lips," a smile that said, "this was well done."[6]

Soon Jesse began hearing from college recruiters. In the years after the Great Depression, fewer than

Proud members of Jesse Owens's family gathered with him on June 27, 1933. Back row (from left to right): Aunt Addie, Quincy, Laverne, Hazel, Lillian, Josephine. Front row: father Henry Cleveland Owens, Pearline, Jesse, mother Emma Owens.

fifteen out of every one hundred students went on to college. Colleges did not have money to offer athletes. Instead, they found them jobs to help pay for tuition, room, board, and books. Owens weighed his options. He chose Ohio State University in Columbus. He would be the first Owens child to go to college.

Before Jesse Owens left high school, Charles Riley handed him a well-worn copy of a poem written by Henry Wadsworth Longfellow. The poem's title, "Excelsior," means "Ever Upward" in Latin.[7]

5

THE BUCKEYE BULLET

 hen he got to Ohio State in October, Jesse Owens's first problem was finding a place to live. Because he was African American, Owens was not permitted to live in the one men's dorm. Most of OSU's fourteen thousand students lived off campus. Owens moved into a boardinghouse where other African-American students lived.

The separation of races did not end there. African Americans could not eat in the restaurants close to campus. Owens and his housemates cooked their own meals or ate at the student union. Only one Columbus movie theater admitted African Americans, but they had to sit in the back six rows of the balcony.

Race also affected the job that the track department had found for Owens at the state capitol building in Columbus. White athletes ran the front elevators that people rode to work. Black athletes mopped floors and did other menial jobs. Owens ran the freight elevator on the night shift. While this unequal treatment angered others, Owens made the best of the situation. At night, the freight elevator took the cleaning crew from floor to floor, only once every hour. So for the rest of his shift, Owens studied.

Away from home for the first time, Owens struggled with his classes. By the second quarter of his freshman year, Owens's low grades put him on academic probation.

His academic troubles did not hurt his status as an athlete. Early in 1934, the Amateur Athletic Union elected Owens to the All-America Track and Field Team. To help pay for school expenses, track coach Larry Snyder arranged for Owens to visit schools and civic groups. This was quite an honor for a freshman. Columbus residents were avid sports fans. They welcomed a visit from Ohio's "meteor of the sprint world."[1] During these visits, Owens, a natural storyteller, talked about the school's sports programs and races he had won. Slowly, he corrected his poor grammar and polished his speaking style.

Owens also worked part time in the college library and cleared tables in the cafeteria. He regularly sent money home to his mother and to Ruth Solomon. The time these jobs took didn't help his schoolwork.

Owens worked out at the track to stay in shape for the spring track season. He began to train with track coach Larry Snyder. In his second year as head coach, Snyder was only ten years older than Owens and a former OSU track star himself. Snyder had a ready smile and a get-down-to-business attitude.

Snyder knew that other coaches were watching to see how he handled Jesse Owens. The chance to work with such a gifted athlete was the hope and prayer of every track coach. Snyder wanted Owens to make faster starts. His arm action needed some work, too. Snyder wanted Owens to smooth out his rhythm and relax his upper body. In the long jump, Snyder trained Owens to kick his feet, as if he were running in mid-air. This "hitch-kick" helped push him farther forward before he landed. Snyder also had Owens shadowbox—that is, box with an imaginary opponent—to improve his footwork and jumping.

Snyder said Owens was easy to coach because he listened well and was eager to train. Snyder said Owens had a finely tuned nervous system, the stuff of champions.

Owens trusted Snyder's judgment and tried to put his advice into practice. The two spent as many hours

At Ohio State University, Jesse Owens's coach was Larry Snyder (right), a former OSU track star himself. The two became lifelong friends.

in the coach's office as they did on the track. Snyder talked to Owens about "keeping his feet on the ground and not letting himself get stuck up and strutting a cakewalk."[2] Sometimes these "sermons" got so intense that they both ended up with tears streaming down their faces. Snyder and Owens became lifelong friends.

Ohio State freshmen were not allowed to compete in varsity meets. But during his first track season in the spring of 1934, Owens took part in several open meets and exhibitions. Twice, he ran against Ralph Metcalfe of Marquette University. Owens lost both times. However, he did set personal conference records for freshmen in the 100-yard dash, the 220-yard sprint, and the long jump.

At the end of his freshman year, he returned home to Cleveland—to his family, home cooking, and Ruth and their child. That summer, Owens took part in community and church picnics and sports carnivals. As he said later, "Being in motion—moving—was always what made me tick . . . I hated to sit or to stand still."[3] At night, he pumped gas at Alonzo Wright's Sohio service station, where he had worked for several summers.

In his sophomore year at Ohio State, Owens worked as a page, running errands in the state senate. The indoor track season lasted from February through March. Packed into crowded cars, the athletes traveled to meets and special events. Once they arrived, the white athletes went to hotels. Black athletes stayed at the YMCA or on special floors of the hotels, where they used the freight elevator. This unequal treatment caused strain and tension.

During the outdoor track season, from April through June, Owens raced against other rising young track stars. At one meet, he finally beat Ralph Metcalfe. Others he raced against were Ben Johnson, of Columbia University, and Eulace Peacock, of Temple University. Students, Columbus fans, and news reporters began to call Owens the "Buckeye Bullet." (Ohio State's sports teams were called the Buckeyes, after the state tree.)

The key event of that school year came on May 25, 1935, at the Big Ten Track and Field Championships in Ann Arbor at the University of Michigan. A few weeks before, Owens had fallen and injured his back. Each day the pain got worse, moving from his back into the hamstring muscles of his thighs.

On the day before the pre-race trials, Owens soaked in a hot whirlpool bath. Snyder almost scratched Owens from the roster but later said that any injury that didn't come from running could not be hurt by running. Owens made it through the qualifying heats.

Through the night, he covered his sore muscles with hot packs. Slowly, the pain eased. Saturday dawned, a perfect sunny spring day for the meet. A gentle wind blew at the runners' backs. Trainers had warmed Owens's body with a red pepper rub and had smeared wintergreen on his legs. He lined up for the 100-yard dash. Though winning was on his mind, his muscles still ached. Owens's pain melted away as soon as the race began. When the handheld stopwatch clicked, Owens's time of 9.4 seconds had tied the world record. Records were harder to set in those days. A time was not clocked until a runner's torso crossed the finish line.

A few minutes later, Owens got ready for the long jump. When Owens's turn came, he ran smoothly down the runway and kicked off the board into the air. Ralph Young, Michigan State's athletic director, remembered Owens soaring past, his feet even with Young's head. (Young was five feet eight inches tall.) Owens landed 26 feet 8¼ inches (8.13 meters) from where he had begun. He had set a new world record. Applause and cheering rippled through the crowd.

Another world record fell a few minutes later. Owens ran the 220-yard sprint in 20.3 seconds. By now, the crowd knew something rare was unfolding. A hush fell over the stadium when Owens lined up for his last event, the 220-yard hurdles. Owens's stride was only seven feet long. This meant he had to leap faster and farther over the hurdles than longer-legged hurdlers. When the race ended, the roar from the crowd

Ohio State still displays this tribute to one of Jesse Owens's greatest days. At the Big Ten Track and Field Championships in Ann Arbor, Michigan, on May 25, 1935, Owens smashed three world records and tied a fourth.

sounded like an airplane on takeoff. Owens had broken the world record for the 220-yard hurdles with a time of 22.6 seconds. In just 45 minutes, Owens had smashed three world records and tied a fourth.

Owens later called that day the "biggest day I've ever had."[4] Larry Snyder said of Owens's running style, "There is no pounding of the track when he runs; his feet kiss the track like a billiard ball when it clicks; he doesn't bruise the cinders."[5]

Sitting in the stands, white-haired Charles Riley shed tears of joy at his former student's success. After the meet, a crush of reporters and fans surrounded Owens. Once he reached the locker room, Owens quickly showered and dressed. To avoid the crowd, he climbed out a back window. Riley waited outside the stadium, his Model T running. The two chugged through the night to reach Cleveland by early Sunday morning. After breakfast, the Owenses' neighbors and friends stopped over. So did reporters. Writer Jack Clowser, who had followed Owens since junior high, said of him, "A courteous and modest gentleman makes the best world champion, and Cleveland should be proud of him [Owens]."[6]

Many track experts still think of May 25, 1935, in Ann Arbor as one of the greatest one-day performances in the history of track and field. That day put Owens's name into the world track and field record books. His life would never be the same again.

6

EYES ON BERLIN

fter Jesse Owens's triumph in Ann Arbor, fans flocked to see him. Coach Snyder urged Owens to be a model of good manners and a spokesperson for good race relations. This came naturally to Owens, now twenty-one, though he sometimes tired of "living in a glass bowl."[1] Children wrote him asking for advice about track. In early June 1935, he spent time with Ruth and Gloria, age three. Then he went to California with the OSU team.

In the next two weeks, Owens took part in ten events. He won first place in all of them. Owens beat

Eulace Peacock in both the 100-meter dash and the long jump. West Coast reporters wrote that he soared over barriers and ran with a quiet, relaxed ease.

California crowds clamored for Owens's autograph. Movie stars greeted him. Sometimes, he ran into the locker room to avoid eager fans.

Fame also brought distractions. Women constantly pursued him. In search of any story, true or not, photographers followed Owens. Stories filled with rumors about him and the daughter of a wealthy Los Angeles businessman soon splashed across the pages of eastern newspapers.

By the time Jesse reached Lincoln, Nebraska, with the team, he had received a call from Ruth. No one knows what she said when they finally talked, but Jesse said later that Ruth understood once he explained the truth to her.[2] Still, Owens was not at his best in the meet. He lost to Eulace Peacock and Ralph Metcalfe in the 100 meters, and to Peacock in the long jump.

Jesse hurried home to Cleveland after the meet. On July 5, 1935, Jesse Owens married Ruth Solomon before a minister in the Solomons' living room. This time, everyone knew about the wedding. The couple spent their wedding night at Ruth's parents' home. Early the next morning, Jesse boarded a train bound for Buffalo, New York. He had already planned to compete in track meets there and in Canada.

In his next three track meets, he again lost to

Eulace Peacock in the 100-yard dash. Thrown together in meet after meet, the two became friends. People talked about both as Olympic prospects.

For the rest of the summer, Jesse ran in track meets and pumped gas in Cleveland. As his junior year at Ohio State approached, Owens's amateur status came into question. Over the summer, the Ohio Legislature had paid Jesse $159 to work as an honorary page, even though he used the money to travel and compete with the track team. The Amateur Athletic Union (AAU) said Owens had broken a rule by taking the money when he wasn't actually working as a page.

The AAU threatened to ban Owens from competing on the track team. Even though he gave the money back, the debate dragged on into the fall. Eventually, the uproar quieted. Jesse could compete after all. He returned to Ohio State for his junior year. Ruth and little Gloria joined him in Columbus.

A second problem that fall dealt with world politics. The 1936 Olympics would take place in Berlin, Germany. German dictator Adolf Hitler had founded the Nazi party and seized power in 1933. Since then, Hitler had taken away the civil rights of German Jews and other groups he didn't consider worthy of his "master race." Because of Hitler's racist views, the U.S. Olympic Committee was talking about boycotting the games.

Some people in the United States did not believe

the stories about Hitler. Others said it did not make sense to boycott Hitler for excluding people. After all, they argued, in parts of the United States, African Americans had to drink from separate drinking fountains. On buses, they rode in the back. In some southern states, African Americans could not vote. Major league baseball and football players were all white. The debate about Hitler's Olympics posed a tough choice for African-American athletes. They felt torn between the issue of racism and a chance many had worked for all their lives.

On a radio show, Jesse Owens said the United States should not take part in the games if Hitler kept up his racist actions. Coach Larry Snyder felt that if Owens did not go to the 1936 Olympics, his moment in history might never come again.

Owens worked hard at his jobs, his training, and his studies. But when fall quarter grades arrived, he had another problem. Because he had failed a class, he could not compete with the track team during winter quarter.

For the next few months, Jesse focused on his schoolwork and trained hard on his own. He also spoke to young people at high schools and colleges and did radio programs on physical fitness.

He traveled with the team to a few meets. During a couple of these road trips, restaurants barred Owens and the other African Americans on the team from

Even when Jesse Owens could not compete with the Ohio State team, he never gave up. He continued to train hard.

entering. Dave Albritton flew into a rage when one owner smashed his fist into a plate of food, saying he would not serve food to African Americans. Owens talked his friend out of making a fuss. The experience left them feeling shaken and empty inside.[3]

During one non-college meet at a Cleveland Public Hall, Jesse Owens showed he could be fair and gracious under pressure. Owens, Eulace Peacock, and two others lined up on makeshift starting blocks for a 50-yard dash. (Only recently had starting blocks begun to be used for some races.) When the race began, Owens shot forward. Peacock's starting block slipped and he stumbled. Instead of running, he watched as Owens easily won the race. Owens insisted they begin again. Peacock won this time. Owens lost the race but won his fans' respect.

By spring quarter, Owens had raised his grades enough to rejoin the team. If he wanted to go to the Olympics, he knew he would have to race his way back to the top. He had run six major races since July 1935. Eulace Peacock had won first place in all of them.

The two runners were to compete again at the Penn Relays in April. But during the semifinals for the 400-meter relay, Peacock pulled a hamstring muscle, a serious injury. Owens, without his best rival, easily won the 100-meter and long jump, and anchored the relay team to victory.

Owens could not have wished for a better spring

season. In the next five meets, he broke world, conference, and local meet records. He ran the 100-yard dash in 9.4 seconds, equaling the world mark he had tied at Ann Arbor.

In mid-July 1936, Olympic tryout finals took place at Randall's Island, New York. Ten African-American men made the track and field team. Jesse Owens, Ralph Metcalfe, and Mack Robinson (older brother of Jackie Robinson) were among the sprinters. Cornelius Johnson and Dave Albritton made the team in the high jump. Sadly, Eulace Peacock never fully recovered from his hamstring injury. Olympic history might have been different if he had.

Jesse Owens was not the only African-American athlete making the news. Boxer Joe Louis, the "Brown Bomber," had beaten every opponent who came his way. Six weeks before the Berlin Olympics, the German boxer Max Schmeling beat Joe Louis and won the heavyweight championship of the world. For Hitler and his believers, Schmeling's victory served as good proof of his warped view that Northern European whites (Aryans) were superior human beings.

The main hopes of African Americans now rested on Jesse Owens. He set his sights on the Olympics in Berlin. The most momentous event of his life lay straight ahead.

7

A MAGNIFICENT DISPLAY

 n July 15, 1936, reporters, photographers, and well-wishers buzzed around America's 384 Olympic athletes as they boarded the S.S. *Manhattan*. With lights flashing and a blast from its horn, the ship steamed out of the harbor, bound for the eleventh Olympiad in Berlin.

Dressed neatly in a dark blue pinstripe suit, Jesse Owens, twenty-two, watched the skyline of New York City slowly shrink, then vanish. Soon all he saw were silvery ocean waves beneath the sky's blue bowl. He had left behind everything familiar and important— Ruth, young Gloria, his parents, sisters, and brothers.

Ahead lay what he had worked for ever since those early-morning training sessions with Charles Riley.

Housed in two decks below the waterline, the athletes settled into a routine. They played shuffleboard and cards. They wrote letters and read. Each day they stretched, jogged, and walked around the deck—light exercise compared to their usual training routines. Delighted with the rich food served on board, some athletes overate and gained weight.

Cold, drizzly weather in Berlin made it hard for the athletes to practice and compete in the preliminary trials. Here, Jesse Owens (right) huddles with other runners: (left to right) American Frank Wykoff, Swiss Paul Hanni, and American Ralph Metcalfe.

Owens wrote in his diary and slept to combat homesickness, boredom, and anxiety. His OSU coach Larry Snyder had come along on the trip, but not as an official coach. Snyder calmed Owens's pre-Olympics jitters. Fellow sprinter Ralph Metcalfe, a veteran of the 1932 team, also told Owens what to expect in the days ahead.

Once in Berlin, the American athletes paraded down the city's main street. Thousands of Germans cheered. Nazi flags flew from every shop, home, and street corner. The flag, with its bold black swastika, was the symbol of the Nazi party. The city sparkled. Hitler's anti-Jewish posters and graffiti had all vanished.

In previous weeks, the Nazi-controlled German newspapers had run stories hinting that the United States teams would be helped by the "black legions."

"We were everything Hitler hated," Jesse said.[1] He and the rest of the track team wondered how much power Hitler had in reserve in his blond, blue-eyed super athletes.

Hitler had built a beautiful Olympic village to house the five thousand athletes from fifty-three nations. The village had a library, hospital, theater, barber, shops, swimming pool, and practice fields. In the mammoth restaurant, ninety cooks prepared meals for every taste. Owens loved the food.[2]

Owens met people from all over the world. "Sitting

around listening to a Victrola having a bull session with some of the boys," he wrote in his diary.[3] Owens roomed with Dave Albritton. At night, they lay awake plotting how Albritton could beat his teammate Cornelius Johnson in the high jump.

The games would begin in one week. Most teams had arrived early to allow time for practice. Ducking in and out of rain showers, the track and field team practiced. Each day, Larry Snyder worked with Owens and Albritton. Snyder worried that Jesse's one pair of track shoes might wear out before the games were over.[4] With his own money, Snyder bought Jesse a new pair.

In spite of their leader's racist views, the German people loved Jesse Owens. Fans asked for autographs. Young boys and girls mobbed him, hoping to shake his hand. Women sent him perfumed love letters and marriage proposals, not caring that he was already married.

Opening Day ceremonies took place on August 1, 1936. Shortly before noon, one hundred and ten thousand spectators entered the Olympic stadium. Trumpets announced the entry of Adolf Hitler. Dressed in his Nazi uniform, Hitler strutted down the steps. The crowd rose and shouted "*Heil Hitler* [Hail Hitler]" and gave the Nazi salute—right arm stretched out and up, open hand, palm down. Hitler entered his special viewing box. Members of the International

Olympic Committee joined him. Some of the other Germans who sat with Hitler—Goering, Goebbels, Hess—would later become known as Hitler's evil henchmen.

A huge orchestra and three thousand singers performed works by famous German composers such as Beethoven and Handel. The German national anthem, "Deutschland Uber Alles," played. The "Olympic Hymn," by composer Richard Strauss, followed. As the notes faded, the sixteen-ton Olympic bell pealed.

Then the athletes marched in, led by a flag bearer and dressed in the uniforms of their countries. Members of each delegation paid their respects to Hitler according to the custom of their country. Some countries gave the Olympic salute. Because it was similar to the Nazi salute, the crowd mistook it for that and cheered wildly. The Americans saluted by placing their white straw hats over their hearts and turning their heads "eyes right"—so they faced Hitler. All the countries except one dipped their flags when they passed Hitler's box. The Americans had made it clear: the United States flag dipped for no one.

Next came the German delegation, dressed in white and marching eight abreast. German fans stood, their arms jutting out in the Nazi salute. After months of training, the six hundred athletes had been chosen from elite sports clubs. Hitler had banned Jewish

Whenever Germany's dictator, Adolf Hitler (right), appeared in the Olympic stadium, crowds gave the Nazi salute and shouted "*Heil* [hail] *Hitler.*" Because of Hitler, millions of Jews and other "enemies" of his Third Reich died during World War II.

youths from taking part in these sports clubs. That way, Jews had no chance of making the German team. Hitler had given a clear message to his athletes. He wanted complete victory—political and athletic. Olympic medals would help prove his theory of racial superiority.

With over five thousand athletes massed on the field before him, Hitler proclaimed the games of the eleventh Olympiad officially open. On cue, thousands of doves fluttered skyward. They swirled and swooped over the stadium.

Then came the final moment of drama. Blaring trumpets sounded. The runner bearing the Olympic torch entered the stadium. Tall, muscular, blond, and white, he was Hitler's idea of a perfect human being. Holding the torch high, he loped around the track. As he ran, Handel's "Hallelujah Chorus" played. Nimbly, the runner climbed the steps to the ten-foot-high "altar" above the marathon gate. Here the Olympic flame would burn for the next two weeks. The runner held the torch to the huge bowl, and flames leaped into the sky.

Jesse Owens later declared Hitler's opening ceremony "a magnificent display."[5] The storm clouds of war were massing worldwide. Yet, according to Owens, for one brief moment the athletes basked in the warm bond that ignored race and country. The Olympic stadium became an island apart from the storm.

8

THE 1936 OLYMPICS

n the days leading up to the 1936 Olympics, Owens struggled to get used to the German starting signals.

"Auf die platze! [On your mark!]" Each runner settled into position. One knee rested on the ground. The other leg stretched out behind.

"Fertig! [Set!]" The runners rose up into a half-crouched position, extended fingers touching the track. Their legs tensed. *Bang!* A man standing close behind the runners sounded the starting gun. Runners lurched forward, digging into the track with their needle-spiked shoes.

To qualify for the 100-meter race, Owens ran three preliminary races. African-American teammate Ralph Metcalfe also qualified. He had almost won the gold medal in the 100-meter race in 1932.

The final 100-meter race took place on a drizzly, cold afternoon in Berlin. Owens and the other runners used trowels to scoop "toe holds" out of the soggy, red cinder track. (Starting blocks were not yet used in the Olympics.)

"This is it," Owens thought. "A lifetime of training for just 10 seconds."[1]

"Auf die platze!"

"Fertig!"

The starting gun boomed. Owens bolted out in front with the power of a cyclone. Ralph Metcalfe put on a burst of speed toward the end of the race. Still, Owens crossed the finish line ahead of Metcalfe. Third place went to Martinus Osendarp of Holland.

Owens had tied the world and Olympic records of 10.3 seconds. Afterward, he spoke with reporters. A broad grin crinkled his face as photographers snapped pictures. Sounding like a courtly gentleman, he said: "I'm very glad to have won the 100 meters in the Olympic Games here in Berlin. It's a beautiful place, a beautiful city. The competition was grand. But I was very glad to come out on top. Thank you very kindly."[2]

Proudly, Owens stood on the winner's platform for the Olympic ceremony. Each medalist wore a laurel wreath (a symbol of victory) around his head. Winners received their gold, silver, or bronze medals. They were also given a foot-high live oak tree. Owens had one thought in his mind as the United States national anthem played. He was an Olympic champion. Hitler watched the scene from his box, his face a stony mask.

The day before, Hitler had greeted and praised all other gold medal winners from Germany and Finland. But when African-Americans Cornelius Johnson and

With the toes of his track shoes sunk into holes dug in the cinder track, Jesse Owens waited for the boom of the starting gun for the 100-meter dash. He tied the world and Olympic records; fellow African-American Ralph Metcalfe came in second.

Dave Albritton won first and second in the high jump, Hitler left the stadium before the U.S. national anthem played. The Olympic committee told Hitler he had to greet all medal winners or none. After that, Hitler congratulated no one in public. American newspaper headlines blared, "Hitler Ignores Negro Medalists." Other newspapers expanded the story into "Hitler Snubs Jesse."[3]

Owens said later, "We lost no sleep over not being greeted by Adolf Hitler."[4] The crowd chanted Owens's name whenever he walked onto the field. Sometimes he entered the stadium through secret passageways to avoid eager fans.

Each athlete had three tries to qualify in the long jump. When Owens took a practice run, judges counted that as his first attempt. On his second try, he stepped over the front edge of the takeoff board from which jumpers leaped into the air. Judges called this a foul. In previous meets, Owens had already jumped twenty-six feet. None of the other jumpers had done that. Panic gnawed at him; his nerves jangled.[5]

Suddenly Luz Long, a blond-haired, blue-eyed German jumper, came up to Owens. As Owens told the story, Long suggested that Owens place a marker a foot back of the foul line. That way, he would not overrun the takeoff board. Thanks to Long's advice, Owens easily qualified on his third jump.

In the finals, Owens watched Long take his first jump. As he ran toward the takeoff board, Long's legs pumped up and down, like an engine's pistons. Then he jumped into the air, like an eagle rising above a mountain, Owens said. Long's jump measured over twenty-five and a half feet. Owens's first jump measured two inches farther. Long's second jump tied that distance. The two jumpers kept bettering or matching each other until it was time for Owens's final jump.

"I had one jump left," said Owens. "I wanted it to be remembered."[6]

Owens ran with long, loping strides toward the takeoff board and leaped into the air. In his mind he was floating, weightless, reaching for the clouds. One American writer said Owens looked as if he were "jumping clear out of Germany."[7] When Owens felt himself falling back down, he fought it. He kicked his legs and moved his arms to gain extra inches. When he finally hit the ground, sand flew up against his face and legs. Owens had won the gold medal and set a new Olympic record with a jump of 8.06 meters (26 feet 5½ inches).

The first person to come up to Owens was Luz Long, who had won the silver medal. He raised Owens's arm and shouted his name to the crowd in his German accent, "Jazze Owenz!" The crowd chanted it, too. Owens and Long walked arm in arm past Hitler's viewing box.

"Hitler must have gone crazy watching us embrace," Owens said later.[8]

That night, the two sat up late in the Olympic village drinking coffee and talking. Owens knew no German and Long spoke only limited English. They communicated as well as they could. The same age, both had grown up poor. Both were married and had one child. Like Owens, Long worried about his future after the Olympics. Owens explained what it was like in America for people of color. Long said he did not agree with Hitler's racist views and actions. As they talked, an easy friendship formed. Owens explained it later by saying, "We both believed in the possibilities of a man to make something of himself and his world."[9]

The next day, Owens boarded the shuttle bus with the other athletes for the fifteen-mile ride to the stadium. By the time they reached the stadium, the damp cold had turned to rain. Owens easily qualified for the 200-meter race.

Hitler arrived with his usual flourish to attend the finals that afternoon. His open black limousine slowly glided through the Berlin streets to the stadium. Cheers and rhythmic chants—"*Sieg heil! Sieg heil!* [hail to victory]"—rippled through the crowd. Hitler's darting eyes scanned the crowd, the tiny black brush of a mustache on his unsmiling face. Once in the stadium, Hitler watched the events intently. Sometimes he rocked back and forth in his seat.

With a flying leap, Owens won the gold medal and set a new Olympic record in the long jump.

Up until August 5, African Americans had won medals in eight different events, including four of the five gold medals for the United States. The Nazi newspaper ran a story that called the team's African Americans "a black auxiliary force [a second-rate support group for the team]." One angry German official complained about the Americans' using "non-humans, like Owens and other Negro athletes."[10]

Most of the German fans did not feel the same way, especially about Owens. People marveled at his smooth running motion and record-smashing speed. They wanted to feel his muscles. They poked cameras in his face. Even German soldiers wanted Owens's autograph.

Everyone knew Owens was trying for his third gold medal in the 200-meter race. His biggest threat in this race was fellow African-American Mack Robinson.

"*Auf die platze!*" came the now familiar words.

"*Fertig!*" Owens and the other runners moved into position. When the starting gun sounded, Owens sprang forward. Mack Robinson did, too. When Robinson crossed the finish line, he had broken a record set by Eddie Tolan in 1932. Robinson had come in second, five-tenths of a second too slow. Owens won the 200-meter race with an Olympic-record-setting time of 20.7 seconds.

The crowd jumped to their feet and applauded. The last time anyone had won three gold medals in one Olympics was 1900. Thomas Wolfe, an American writer from the South, whooped and hollered so loudly that Hitler turned and glared at him.

"Owens was black . . . but what the hell, it was our team, and I thought he was wonderful," said Wolfe.[11] His words showed the mixed feelings some white Americans had toward their black countrymen. Even glowing magazine articles in the 1930s contained racist comments and terms that are not acceptable today.

Prejudice also entered into the choosing of the 400-meter relay team for the race to be held on August 8. Track coaches had planned to have runners Marty Glickman and Sam Stoller as part of the four-man team. Instead, a few days before the race, coaches announced that Jesse Owens and Ralph Metcalfe would join Californians Foy Draper and Frank Wykoff. Some said it was because Owens and Metcalfe had done so well. Another theory was that the Americans did not want to irritate Hitler by including Glickman and Stoller, who were both Jewish, on the relay team. Stoller and Glickman protested.

"*Any* of our runners," said Glickman, "the milers or the hurdlers could run against the Germans or anyone else and win by fifteen yards."[12]

When the coach announced the change, Owens said, "I've won three gold medals. Let Marty and Sam have their chance." The coach ordered Owens to do as he was told.[13] Owens later said of the decision, "It was the politics of our own American officials [not Hitler or the Germans] that kept them [Glickman and Stoller] off the team."[14]

In a 400-meter relay, each team member runs 100 meters. When the first runner finishes his part of the race, he passes the baton to the next runner, waiting ahead in the lane. As the lead-off man, Jesse Owens sped the first 100 meters, setting a fast pace. Metcalfe, waiting up ahead, grabbed the baton and shot forward. His powerful, long legs increased the Americans' lead. Draper carried the baton around the curve, and Wykoff streaked first across the finish line. The Americans set a world-record time of 39.8 seconds. The German team was a distant second, the Italian team third.

The relay team wanted Owens to stand on the top step of the winners' platform. But Owens demanded that Metcalfe have the honor. Three times before, Metcalfe had narrowly missed winning a gold medal. Now Owens wanted Metcalfe to enjoy this moment.

On August 16, the 1936 Olympics ended. Artists chiseled Jesse Owens's name four times into the stone wall of the stadium, along with the other winners' names. To Hitler's delight, the German athletes had won more medals and team points than any other country. The Americans were second, the Italians third. Still, in track and field events the American athletes had taken twelve gold medals. Four of them belonged to a whirlwind named Jesse Owens.

Owens left the 1936 Olympics with warm memories. He had met athletes from all over the world. He had made new friends, like Luz Long. The athletes had competed. They had also laughed, cried, eaten, and talked together. In three years, many of these young men and women would face off against each other on the front lines of a terrible war.

The Olympic flag fluttered in the wind. Then slowly, it was lowered. The massive Olympic bell echoed. Choirs sang their last notes into the night sky. The Olympic flame flickered and died.

As Owens said later, "There was not one among us who was not moved. We wept without shame."[15]

9

THE EBONY EXPRESS

 esse Owens left Berlin a hero. One newspaper article called him "the god of the sports fans," another, the "ebony express."[1] Hitler's official film producer, Leni Riefenstahl, devoted film footage to Owens in her famous movie *Olympia*. Charmed by Owens's grace and dignity, she thought him symmetrically perfect.[2]

Owens was exhausted. All he wanted to do was go home, but the Amateur Athletic Union, the sponsor of the Olympic athletes, had other plans. It needed money to cover its debts from the Olympics. The AAU had booked a series of track exhibitions in Northern and Eastern Europe to begin right after the Olympics.

Coach Larry Snyder tried to talk Owens out of joining the tour. Snyder said it was not fair to force the athletes to compete so soon. Owens had another reason for not wanting to go. Tempting offers had begun to trickle in. One California orchestra had offered to pay him $25,000 just to appear on stage. The AAU made it clear: Going on the tour was an order. Jesse Owens's presence at the meets would make people buy tickets.

Owens and the rest of the track team hastily packed and boarded a train. Larry Snyder went along, too. At a meet in Prague, Czechoslovakia, Owens won the 100-meter race in 10.7 seconds, his slowest time in months. His winning long jump barely matched his high school record. At one meet, he lost the 100-meter race to Ralph Metcalfe. In spite of his winning spring track season and his four Olympic gold medals, Owens's focus was off. Snyder later said it was because the AAU was "running his [Jesse's] legs off."[3]

From the windows of speeding trains and planes, the athletes caught only glimpses of snow-capped mountains, winding rivers, quaint villages, and unfamiliar sights. Once in a city, they competed before huge crowds. Sometimes a banquet followed that lasted until midnight. The next morning, the team hurried off to a new city and another contest. Snyder

When the 1936 Olympics ended, Jesse Owens's name, along with those of other champions, was etched into the stadium wall.

complained that the AAU was treating the athletes like "trained seals" and using Jesse for "bait." Some quipped, "We are running to pay for the potatoes we ate in the village."[4]

The group arrived in London, England. Owens and most of the other athletes were broke. With no money to buy souvenirs or see the sights, they wandered London's streets on foot. Or they gathered in the hotel lobby to play games for pennies and wooden matches.

Owens had a serious talk with Coach Snyder. Should Owens leave the tour and grab his chance to make big money? What about finishing college? Snyder knew if Owens did not return for his senior year, Ohio State would lose the heart of its track team. But Owens's future and security were more important.

Snyder, who considered Owens the "world's greatest track athlete,"[5] had told a reporter, "It would be foolish for me to stand in Jesse's way. He's absolutely at the height of his fame now. Nothing that he could do in his remaining year of college competition would lift him to a higher peak in the athletic world than he now enjoys."[6]

Sitting in on the talk between Owens and Snyder were other sports officials and college coaches. They, too, felt locked in a power struggle with the AAU, which often had the final say over college athletes.

Finally, the group advised Jesse Owens to drop out of the tour and return early to the United States. Soon after, an agent offered to pay Owens $40,000 to appear with a popular song-and-dance man. Other offers arrived—to be in the movies, even to be a college track coach and teacher after graduation. Owens telegraphed his wife and parents: He was coming home.

Jesse Owens competed in one more meet in the London stadium before he dropped out of the tour. The American track team did well against a joint English and Canadian team. Ten records in fourteen different events were broken, including four world records. Jesse Owens competed in only one race, a four-man relay. The relay team won, but Owens's heart was not in it.

The next day, the track team left for Sweden without Owens. An AAU official called Snyder and demanded that Owens board the next plane for Stockholm. Snyder bristled. He said this was Owens's big chance. Within hours, the head of the Amateur Athletic Union announced that Owens was suspended—indefinitely— from competing as an amateur.

Snyder accused the AAU of thinking only about its cut of the ticket sales. Owens complained to reporters, "This track business is becoming one of the biggest rackets in the world. . . . A fellow desires something for himself."[7]

On August 19, Snyder and Owens boarded a luxury ocean liner, the *Queen Mary*. Just before the ship sailed for New York City, Owens received a $200 check. Alonzo Wright, owner of the Sohio station in Cleveland where Owens had worked, had heard that he was flat broke. Wright and a local barber had pooled their money and wired it to their hometown hero.

As the ship neared New York City, cables began to arrive. Everyone wanted to talk to Jesse Owens— reporters, agents, promoters, fans. Popular African- American tap dancer and nightclub entertainer Bill "Bojangles" Robinson cabled Owens, telling him not to do anything before he saw Robinson.

After Jesse Owens dropped out of the Olympic tour, he competed in one more track meet. He ran in a four-man relay in London. The American relay team won, but Owens's heart was not in it.

Owens's fame did not help his wife, parents, and family when they tried to rent a hotel room in New York City. Several big hotels turned them away because they were African Americans. With the help of an Ohio congressman, they finally found rooms. The next morning they boarded a Coast Guard cutter and motored out to the *Queen Mary*, anchored offshore. Ruth, her pretty face beaming, showered Owens with hugs and kisses.

Once the ship docked, people bustled around Owens. Cameras whirred and clicked. Reporters shouted questions: Why had he quit the tour? Was he angry at Adolf Hitler and the AAU? What would he do now? Owens's former coach and mentor, Charles Riley, also stood in the crowd. Bursting with pride, he watched his former track star give careful, upbeat answers to reporters' questions. When asked about the upcoming presidential election, Owens said he'd vote for whichever candidate would do the most for African Americans.

Then Bill "Bojangles" Robinson whisked Owens and his family away to a party in Owens's honor held at Robinson's apartment in Harlem, an African-American neighborhood in New York City. There he introduced Owens to Marty Forkins. Forkins, Robinson's agent, offered to promote Owens, too.

At Robinson's party, Owens told a reporter he thought that African Americans should have a chance to take part in all professional sports. Unwritten laws kept African Americans out of many sports. Actual laws, known as Jim Crow laws, made the separation of blacks and whites legal, and kept African Americans out of restaurants, hotels, businesses, neighborhoods, and voting booths.

Owens later pointed out that while Hitler had not offered to shake his hand, neither had the President of the United States, Franklin Delano Roosevelt.[8]

10

WELCOME HOME

leveland threw a big welcome party when the Owens family returned. Riding in an open Lincoln convertible, Jesse and Ruth Owens waved to cheering crowds along the parade route. Confetti and streamers rained down on the car. After glowing speeches at city hall, Owens received a gold watch and other gifts from Cleveland fans.

Then it was on to Columbus for another parade, with more speeches and gifts. Finally, Owens met with Larry Snyder and Ohio State's athletic director to talk about Ohio State. The athletic director argued strongly for Owens to finish his senior year. Coach Snyder remained on Owens's side.

Owens had carried home the four tiny live oak trees he'd been given at the Olympics. Owens left one of them to be planted at Ohio State. Of the three remaining trees, he gave one to his mother, one to Cleveland's East Technical High School, and kept one for himself.

A few days after his meeting at Ohio State, Jesse Owens returned to New York to join the rest of the Olympic athletes. Before their ship arrived, Owens signed a contract with entertainment agent Marty Forkins. Forkins would arrange moneymaking appearances for Owens. Owens also announced he would not return to Ohio State that fall for his senior year. College meant a great deal to him, but he and Coach Snyder saw this as the chance of a lifetime.[1]

In New York City's parade for the Olympic athletes, Jesse Owens rode in the lead car of the motorcade. Cheering fans jammed New York City's narrow streets. Horns honked. Long strands of paper, called ticker tape, fluttered down from open office windows.

When the parade rolled through Harlem, the cheering turned lukewarm. Some said it was because Jack Dempsey, former heavyweight champion, sat next to Jesse Owens. Dempsey, who was white, had refused ever to fight a black boxer. Others said the lack of enthusiasm had to do with the order of the cars. Jesse Owens rode in front, but the rest of the black athletes all rode together toward the back of the parade, separated from their white teammates.

During the final ceremony, the mayor of New York, Fiorello H. LaGuardia, introduced Owens as "an American boy." Then he said, "We are all Americans . . . we have no auxiliaries in this country."[2] He was referring to the Nazi claim that the African Americans were "an auxiliary force."

"For a time at least, I was the most famous person in the entire world," Owens said.[3]

Ruth Owens felt both pride and anxiety for her husband.[4] She knew how hard he had worked for this moment. Owens later said of her, "She understood what running—*what being the best at something*—meant to me."[5] Yet instinct warned Ruth Owens that the glib offers of money and jobs might be short-lived.

She was right. Jesse Owens soon found that most of the job offers fizzled as fast as a fire doused with rain. Offers of movie deals, orchestra gigs, and top jobs at big companies turned out to be just overblown talk by people trying to ride the wave of Owens's popularity. According to him, the only real job he was offered was as a Cleveland playground instructor. "There were four gold medals on the broken-down dresser in our bedroom, an oak tree next to the closet, and no money in my wallet."[6]

Owens's mother had once said of him, "Jesse was

always a face boy. . . . When a problem came up, he always faced it."[7]

In the fall of 1936, he did just that. Republican presidential candidate Alf Landon hired Owens to work on his campaign. At political gatherings, Owens flashed his winning smile, shook hands, and signed autographs. In city after city, he told stories about the Olympics and urged people to vote for Alf Landon. In reality, Landon did not stand a chance against the popular incumbent president, Franklin D. Roosevelt. Republicans had hoped that Owens would help bring out the African-American vote. In November, most African Americans voted for Roosevelt, as did the rest of the voting public. Landon lost by a landslide.

"Poorest race I ever ran," Owens, who never considered himself a politician, said later.[8] Working for Landon, Owens earned more than $10,000. Marty Forkins arranged for his client to speak at banquets and appear at ball games and on radio shows. By late fall, Owens had earned an additional $26,000 or more, a huge sum of money for that time. With the money, Owens bought his parents an eleven-room home with new furniture. He also helped pay for places for two of his sisters to live with their families. For Ruth, he bought jewelry, new clothes, and a 1936 Buick. Friends received generous gifts from him. Just before Christmas, he handed Charles Riley the keys to a new blue Chevrolet to replace his aging Model T

Ford. (One story said that Owens only made the down payment and that Riley struggled to make the payments on his teacher's salary.)[9]

In December, an Associated Press sports poll named Jesse Owens the outstanding athlete of 1936. The year before, boxer Joe Louis had won.

Though he had made a great deal of money, Owens still had no steady work. Filled with a strong will to compete, he yearned to run. Then, Marty Forkins arranged for Owens to race against Cuba's fastest athlete, Conrado Rodriques, during halftime at a soccer game.

Once again, the AAU stepped in. The AAU had taken Owens's contract with Forkins as a final sign that Owens had now turned pro. (Owens had yet to race for money.) Rodriques would lose his amateur status if he raced against Owens, a professional. When Owens reached Havana, Cuba, the plan had changed. He was to race a horse named Julio McCaw.

Other athletes—swimmers, baseball players, runners—had already tried this stunt. Crowds loved it. People even bet on the outcome. Deep down, Jesse knew that no one could really beat a racehorse.

On the day of the race, a small crowd cheered as Owens came onto the field. He took his starting position and waited for the signal. Promoters had given Jesse a forty-yard lead over the horse. So, for the first few seconds, he had the track to himself. But soon, he heard the horse's hooves galloping toward him. The animal breathed in whooshing gulps, as the jockey's whip cracked. Even so, Owens finished several yards ahead of the horse. After four months away from the track, he had run the one hundred yards in an amazing 9.9 seconds.

After the race, fans rushed to get Owens's autograph. Then he collected his $2,000 and went home.

He said of the event: "I had four gold medals, but you can't eat four gold medals. There was no television, no big advertising, no endorsements then. Not for a black man, anyway."[10]

Jesse Owens came home from Cuba to yet another disappointment. The James E. Sullivan Trophy, for the outstanding amateur athlete of the year, had gone to Olympic decathlon champion Glenn Morris. Owens had narrowly missed winning the trophy, probably because of his troubles with the AAU.

The golden glow of Jesse's triumph at the Olympics was beginning to fade. A splash of reality had dulled his sense of joy.

11

A Man in Motion

n the years after the Olympics, Jesse Owens did whatever he could to support his family. In January 1937, he took a job as leader of a touring African-American band. When the band opened at the Savoy ballroom in Harlem in New York City, three thousand people came, including jazz great Louis Armstrong and comedian Jimmy Durante. Dressed in a flashy white tuxedo, Jesse Owens looked great up on stage. Owens admitted he "didn't know one note from another." But musicians taught him about timing, showmanship, and how to handle a baton.[1]

Life on the road with a band was far different from traveling to track meets with a team. The band played in one smoky nightclub after another. Sometimes club-goers got into fights, especially when they had been drinking. Owens quickly grew tired of the seedy side of nightclub life. He returned home to Cleveland that summer, having earned an amazing $100,000.

That fall, he started an African-American basket-ball team called the Olympians. Owens and the team

In the fall of 1937, Jesse Owens started an African-American basketball team called the Olympians. The team played against amateur and semi-professional teams.

traveled all over the country, playing against amateur and semi-professional teams. At halftime during the games, Owens talked about his Olympic experiences and wowed the crowds with his sprinting abilities.

The Olympians also played college teams, until the AAU said they could not compete against amateurs. In their first season, the Olympians won all but six of their 142 games. But money problems plagued the team.

Jesse and Ruth now had a second daughter, Beverly, born October 5, 1937. They had remodeled an old home on Westchester Avenue in Cleveland.

During the summer of 1938, Owens organized a touring softball squad called the Olympics. Most of their games took place in Ohio. When not on the road, Owens worked as a Cleveland playground director for $130 a month.

"Being with kids, playing with them and showing them things, sometimes letting them show me, always made me feel good," Owens said.[2] He may not have known it then, but this was a first step toward a lifetime of working with children, something he grew to love.

At the time, watching kids at a playground did not tap enough of Owens's restless energy. Whenever he traveled with the team, he arranged exhibitions to draw fans and promote the games. He raced against professional baseball players. He demonstrated the sprint and the long jump.

In July 1938, he raced a sixty-yard sprint against boxer Joe Louis, who was the first African-American heavyweight champion of the world. Promoters played up the match—"the world's fastest human" (Owens) against the "Brown Bomber" (Louis). Joe Louis won the race, but only because Owens tripped and fell at the start of the race.

In late summer, two businessmen came to Owens with an idea for a chain of dry cleaning stores. To Owens, the Jesse Owens Dry Cleaning Company sounded like a reliable business that would produce steady income for his family.

"I grabbed at it like you grab the baton in a relay race from a man who's almost out of the legal passing zone—just in time," Owens said later.[3] He invested his money and ran a huge ad in the local newspaper: "Speedy 7 Hour Service by the World's Fastest Runner."[4]

Owens left the day-to-day management of the dry cleaning stores to his two partners. He spent most of his time traveling, promoting his baseball team, and racing.

In October, the federal government told Owens that he owed back taxes on part of what he had earned in 1936. He had made the money in the four months after the Olympics but had not reported it. The government threatened to take his house if he didn't pay the back taxes. Owens scrambled to come up with the cash. He went on tour with his basketball team.

Meanwhile, his dry cleaning business failed. Owens blamed the collapse of the stores on his partners.[5] Now he had debts from his failed business, car payments, plus bills for back taxes, unpaid purchases, and loans from friends. By May 1939, Jesse Owens declared bankruptcy. Under this law, he admitted in court that he could not pay his debts. When he told Ruth, she began to cry softly. He told her everything would work out. He had no idea how.

Sick with worry, Owens asked his father for advice.[6] As Owens later told it, first he and Henry Owens prayed together. Then Henry helped Jesse make a plan to repay his debts. Jesse and Henry Owens took this plan to a Cleveland banker, who agreed to lend Owens the money he needed to cover his debts.

To pay off the bank loan, Owens brainstormed more moneymaking schemes. In the summer of 1939, he toured with an African-American baseball team called the Indianapolis Clowns. The Clowns staged stunts and gags during their games to make the audience laugh. Fans loved watching the Clowns almost as much as they did major league baseball.

A few years before, Owens had said racing against a horse in Cuba made him feel sick. But such stunts sold tickets. So at the end of each Clowns game, Owens raced sixty yards against a horse.

On the road with the Clowns, Owens usually followed the team bus in his Buick. The Clowns' manager, Ed Hamman, rode beside him. Hamman, who was white, recalled times in both the South and the North when restaurants refused to serve Owens food. At first when that happened, Hamman said he would not eat there either. Owens shrugged off the insult. He convinced Hamman to bring sandwiches out to the car for them. Bigotry was nothing new. Everything Owens had done since high school had made him a highly visible target for racism.

Several events in 1940 made Jesse Owens take stock of his life. First, he unsuccessfully tried selling clothes for a Cleveland clothing company. Then, in March, his mother, Emma Owens, died at age sixty-four. Owens's buoyant spirit crumpled. He cried for three days.[7] Back in 1936, a Cleveland city councilman had called Emma Owens "the soul and heart of Jesse Owens."[8] Now she was gone.

Owens was almost twenty-seven, an age when many sprinters were past their prime. During the 1940 spring college track season, younger track stars had begun to edge toward Owens's records. Jackie Robinson (Mack's younger brother), a four-sport athlete at UCLA, had already long jumped more than twenty-five feet. People wondered if Robinson would soon overtake Owens's record. Unfortunately, because of World War II, the 1940 Olympics had been canceled, as they would also be in 1944.

Owens also had his family to think about. He and Ruth now had three daughters—Gloria, eight, Beverly, three, and Marlene, one. Marlene had been born April 19, 1939. Owens wanted his children to have nice clothes, toys, and plenty of good food. He had spent most of the money he had made since the Olympics on houses, cars, clothes, and all the other things he did not have as a child.

During the summer of 1940, Owens decided he would finish his college education at Ohio State. He had announced this before; this time he meant it. That fall, he moved his whole family to Columbus.

To help pay for his college expenses, he opened a new dry cleaning store on North High Street near the campus. He also helped Larry Snyder with the track team as an assistant trainer.

In his earlier college years, he had avoided tough subjects in order to stay eligible for track. Now he had to tackle the math and science classes he needed for graduation. Between studying, coaching, running his dry cleaning business, and tending to his family, Owens had little time to spare. He struggled even more with his studies, finding it hard to sit still and concentrate. The college campus was also more unsettled than it had been before. Students hotly debated such topics as race and whether the United States should enter the war already raging in Europe.

Such talk made Owens think of his German friend Luz Long from the 1936 Olympics. He and Long had written letters, exchanging news about sports, their families, and their work. Then Long's letters had stopped. Owens knew Long was probably fighting for Germany.

After not hearing from Luz Long for two years, Owens received a letter on September 25, 1940, from somewhere in the North African desert. His friend said he wrote from a place where there was only "dry sand" and "wet blood." He feared it would be the last letter he would write. He asked Owens to promise that after the war he would seek out Long's wife and new baby. Long wanted Owens to tell his child about the father he never knew and about their friendship. Long signed the letter, "Your Brother, Luz."[9] Sadly, Owens later learned that Luz Long died fighting for Germany in 1943.

In the fall of 1940, his father, Henry Owens, fell gravely ill. Jesse, Ruth, and their daughters hurried back to Cleveland to join the rest of the family. Owens willed his father to live: "I prayed for him to live. But I knew that my prayers wouldn't change it, either." Filled with grief, he strained to hear his father's last words to him, but it did no good. "My father's heartbeat was no more."[10]

World events, not personal tragedies, drew Jesse Owens away from college for the last time. At dawn on December 7, 1941, Japanese fighter planes, bombers, and torpedo planes made a surprise attack on the United States naval base at Pearl Harbor, Hawaii. The terrible news flashed over the telegraph wires—almost twenty-four hundred military personnel dead, eighteen warships and one hundred eighty-seven aircraft lost. President Roosevelt called it a "date which will

Jesse Owens and German jumper Luz Long became good friends during the 1936 Olympics. Long wrote his last letter to Owens from the battlefront of World War II.

live in infamy."[11] Within days, the United States was at war—not only against Japan but against Germany and Italy, too.

Because Jesse Owens had a wife and three children, he could not be drafted as a soldier. Instead the United States Office of Civilian Defense asked him to be part of a national fitness program. Owens willingly traveled around the country and talked with African-American groups about exercise programs, health, and physical fitness. Often he gave track exhibitions or showed films of his races. Now he was paid by the federal government.

He soon moved on to a job well suited to his talents, with the Ford Motor Company in Detroit. Companies that made automobiles had converted to making planes, ships, tanks, jeeps, and artillery for the war effort. Owens became a personnel director, acting as a link to the many African Americans being hired by Ford. He helped newly arrived families find housing, schools, and recreational opportunities. He also worked closely with the Urban League solving problems that arose.

When World War II ended in 1945, soldiers returned to the jobs they had held at Ford before the war. Jesse Owens and many other workers lost their jobs. Owens briefly went into a sporting goods business in Detroit, selling athletic equipment.

In 1947, an exciting breakthrough took place for

African Americans. Jackie Robinson became the first African American to play modern major league baseball. He started at second base for the Brooklyn Dodgers and won rookie of the year honors. With peacetime prosperity came an increase in jobs for white and black workers alike.

Jesse Owens's family had settled into a middle-class neighborhood in Detroit. As always, Owens had bills to pay. After his sporting goods business failed, he toured as a side attraction for the popular Harlem Globetrotters. This African-American basketball team boasted clever, quick-paced routines, with plenty of slapstick humor. For his part, Owens demonstrated his quick starts, gave autographs, mingled with the crowd, and talked about his Olympic experiences.

In 1949, he took a job as a promotional executive with a clothing store on Chicago's west side. The Owens family would move again. For almost fifteen years, Owens had hopscotched from job to job, trying to find the right niche for himself. He later said he may have been driven by the hope that each new experience might turn out to be as fulfilling as the 1936 Olympics had been.

12

AMERICA'S AMBASSADOR

 uth Owens spent much of her time raising her children and making a home for her husband. Still, she did not want to move to Chicago in 1949. Even though her husband's travels often left her alone, she enjoyed living in Detroit. She worked for charities and church groups, helped with her children's activities, played bridge, and joined friends for potluck suppers.

Her three daughters had made friends and liked their schools. They did not want to move, either. Gloria, the eldest daughter, flatly refused to go.

President of her senior class, she wanted to finish high school in Detroit.

The move to Chicago meant a chance for the family to spend more time together, as Owens hoped to base most of his activities there. For Ruth, thirty-four, leaving her oldest daughter behind made the move wrenching. When Ruth finally left with Marlene, ten, and Beverly, twelve, Gloria moved in with a family friend in Detroit.

As the 1950s dawned, the United States sent troops to help South Korea fight North Korea. The Soviet Union and the United States were locked in a hostile standoff called the Cold War. Dwight D. Eisenhower became President of the United States in 1952. These were years when Americans looked for patriotic heroes. Jesse Owens was a positive role model for both black and white citizens. One writer called Owens "a professional good example."[1]

In 1950, the Associated Press named him the greatest track and field athlete in history. At a dinner in Chicago in October, six hundred Chicago businessmen and civic leaders gathered to honor him. Olympic officials and fellow athletes also attended. Ohio State track coach Larry Snyder praised his former superstar, but also gave credit to Ruth Owens for her quiet support. Ralph Metcalfe, Jesse's former Olympic teammate and now a close friend, presented Owens with a plaque. The two played golf regularly.

In 1951, Jesse Owens, thirty-eight, went back to the Olympic stadium in Berlin as part of a Harlem Globetrotters' exhibition. At halftime, a dramatic announcement boomed over the loudspeaker. The "champion of champions" was now entering through the marathon gate. Smiling and waving, Jesse Owens jogged around the track. As he ran by eighty-thousand cheering fans, memories filled every corner of the stadium. He passed the platform of champions, where he and the other winners had received their medals and their laurel wreaths. Other champions had replaced those of 1936. He passed Hitler's empty box. Hitler was now dead, along with the more than 11 million people he had murdered—Jews and others who did not fit his ideal.

After Owens finished his ceremonial "victory lap," the mayor of West Berlin stood and quieted the crowd. Then he said, "Jesse Owens . . . fifteen years ago Hitler refused to shake your hand. I will try to make up for it today by taking both of them." The mayor warmly clasped Jesse's hands. "Jesse Owens, Jesse Owens," the crowd chanted.[2]

During that same visit to Berlin, Owens met Karl, his late friend Luz Long's young son. Owens signed Karl's scrapbook and vowed to keep in contact with him.

Back in Chicago, Owens plunged into working

with boys' clubs, Scout troops, and delinquent youths. He visited schools and talked to kids about sports. He set up swimming programs, field events, and the Junior Sports Jamboree. On the board of directors of the South Side Boys Club, he worked with some fifteen hundred African-American youths. They were eager to talk with Owens, who treated them with patience and respect. Children still wrote him from all over the world. Sometimes they rang his doorbell just to meet him. His work with children gave him great satisfaction. He once said, "The youth of our country, of any country, are the world's greatest resource. . . . It behooves a man with God given ability to stand ten feet tall. You never know how many youngsters may be watching."[3]

In 1953, Owens was appointed Secretary of the Illinois State Athletic Commission. In this job, he supervised amateur and professional boxing matches, establishing safety standards. Once he had organized an all-day amateur boxing program at a school in one of Chicago's poorer areas. He arrived early and found that no American flag flew outside the school. He rummaged around until he found a bedraggled flag. Then he shinnied up the pole to attach the flag at the top. Jesse Owens wanted the American flag flying.

That same year, his daughter Gloria graduated from Ohio State University, the first in the Owens family to earn a college degree. Meanwhile, daughters

Beverly and Marlene were growing up. Beverly became the family rebel. Headstrong and impulsive, she wore outlandish clothes, dyed her hair, and neglected her schoolwork. When her father was home, she toned down these behaviors.

Guiding her daughters through their teenage years was not easy for Ruth Owens. Neither was sharing her husband—her childhood sweetheart—with the rest of the world. Women had always openly flirted with Jesse Owens, drawn by his striking good looks, warm, outgoing nature, and athletic grace. Rumors

Jesse Owens often spoke to groups of Boy Scouts. He also worked with other boys' clubs and helped delinquent youths. He considered the youth of any country its greatest resource.

flew along the gossip grapevine about Jesse and other women. But the Owens's marriage remained strong. Jesse Owens later gave credit to Ruth's devotion, both as a mother and as a wife: "Ruth helped to pull me through a lot, both as a giggly youngster with a sensitivity far beyond her years and as a mature wife who still owns the spirit of youth."[4] Ruth Owens once told an interviewer, "There isn't a greater guy in the world than Jesse Owens. . . . Jesse's trouble is that he's too good."[5] She said Jesse constantly helped friends and strangers and would talk to anybody.

Their daughter Marlene Owens Rankin said the strength of her parents' marriage probably came from their growing up together: "There was a bond between them that most people don't understand."[6]

Jesse Owens's children remember him as a kind, giving person who cared about his family and his home. He brought them gifts from his travels, such as exotic dolls and jewelry. A formal man, he expected good manners and proper dress from his daughters. "You didn't come to breakfast or dinner with your hair in rollers wearing a bathrobe," said Rankin.[7]

Despite his own keen interest in sports, he did not encourage his daughters to take part in competitive sports. Gloria did play high school basketball and was captain of the team. Both Beverly and Marlene took part in grade school sports programs. Marlene Rankin said of her father, "He didn't think it was ladylike to be competitively active, so he didn't encourage our participation, other than as recreation." He also did not feel parents should push their children into sports. "Boys and girls should be involved for the spirit and fun of what team sports teach to all participants."[8]

In 1954, Jesse Owens gave the graduation address at his alma mater, East Technical High School in Cleveland. He talked to the graduates about sports bringing people together.

In 1955, President Eisenhower appointed Jesse Owens a goodwill ambassador for the United States. Owens traveled to the Far East, visiting India, Malaysia, and the Philippines. He was also now a sports specialist for the Illinois Youth Commission. He worked with youth offenders and set up camping, park, and playground activities. Wherever he went, young people crowded around him.

Owens often found it hard to say no to people's requests. He would dash off to meetings, dinners, interviews, and special events, even if he was exhausted. Finally, he realized how little time he was spending with the four people who mattered most to him—his family.

"Like a man caught in quicksand, the harder I struggled, the deeper I sank," he later wrote. Of his daughters, he said, "Too often, I had missed the bittersweet miracle of watching them grow."[9] On one occasion he canceled his travel plans and rushed home thinking that he would get there in time to tuck the little ones into bed. Except that his daughters had grown into women. When he arrived home, Gloria was off at a civil rights meeting. Marlene had an important date. Beverly had a bomb to drop. She wanted to get married. When Jesse protested that she was too young, Ruth just smiled and said, "Look who's talkin'."[10]

Owens vowed to spend more time with Ruth and their daughters, but the Owens nest soon emptied. Marlene Owens followed her sister's path to Ohio State in 1956. Not long after that, Beverly married Donald Prather after completing a year of college.

President Eisenhower again called on Jesse Owens in 1956, asking him and several other athletes to represent the President at the Olympics in Melbourne, Australia. Owens watched the American relay team break his team's 1936 record. The Australian hosts praised Owens's warm, outgoing manner and the way he understood the problems of young people.

In the spring of 1960, Jesse Owens went to Los Angeles, supposedly on Olympic business. To his surprise, he became a guest on one of the most popular television shows of the time—Ralph Edwards's *This Is Your Life*. Jesse Owens sat up on stage. One by one, he heard familiar voices from behind the stage curtain. With the help of Ruth Owens, Edwards had arranged for family, friends, Larry Snyder, and Olympic teammates to honor Jesse Owens and talk about his life.

Even Charles Riley, now aged and feeble, paid tribute to his famous track student. Over the years, Owens had lost touch with the longtime junior high coach and teacher. Riley had previously expressed bitterness about that. Still the reunion in California was one of the highlights of Riley's later years. Riley once said of Owens's Olympic feat, "I never doubted for a moment he would do it. I found him, not just a boy who ran 220 yards for me in 24.7 seconds as a seventh grader, but a boy who yearned for every bit of instruction I could give him and who was always the last to quit practice."[11] Riley had said that in becoming a great runner, Owens developed "the cleanest, swiftest, knifelike thrust I ever hoped to see."[12]

That summer, Owens went to the Olympics in Rome, Italy, to watch Larry Snyder coach the 1960 Olympic track and field team. African-American Ralph Boston broke Owens's last remaining Olympic record, in the long jump. (Owens's records for the 200-meter, 100-meter, and 400-meter relay had already fallen.) By now, Jesse Owens, forty-seven, had accepted an inevitable truth. Records are made to be broken.

Ruth and Jesse Owens returned to Columbus that fall to see their daughter Marlene crowned Ohio State's first African-American homecoming queen. Jesse Owens told his daughter, "Remember Darling, it could only happen in America."[13]

In the fall of 1960, Jesse and Ruth Owens returned to Ohio State University to see their daughter crowned homecoming queen.

That same fall, Owens received the sad news that Charles Riley had died. Riley had been the first to sense raw talent in a skinny, sickly boy and to use it to mold him into a great athlete. Riley's simple tactics—early morning workouts, lessons about life and running, Sunday dinners, trips to track meets in the Model T—had delivered a clear message to the young boy. Riley believed in Jesse Owens.

"It was he who saw my potential when I was hardly healthy enough to run to the corner for a newspaper," said Owens.[14] He said Riley was the man "who made all the difference in his life."[15]

13

"LIFE HAS BEEN GOOD TO ME"

n his later years, Jesse Owens traveled some two hundred and fifty thousand miles a year, endorsing products and doing public relations for major companies. Through the Atlantic Richfield Company (ARCO), Owens began the Jesse Owens Games—for boys and girls interested in track.

"Jesse couldn't stay still," said film producer Bud Greenspan, who has produced the official films for several Olympics. "He was running thirty years after he stopped running."[1]

Owens was a popular speaker at sports banquets,

graduations, churches, businesses, and civic groups. Dressed in well-tailored suits, he stood before the podium with shoulders squared. More important than his words was his dramatic, moving voice. He never used a written text, preferring to offer his ideas on the spur of the moment. He always spoke about familiar themes—the value of family, religion, hard work, patriotism, and the damage that bigotry can do.

"Jesse was a great speechmaker," said Greenspan. "He could make a stone cry."[2]

Like an actor, Owens thrived on the applause of the crowds. He felt he owed it to his fans to shake hands, sit through long dinners, and flash his warm smile. When signing autographs, he always asked the person's name. Then, in neat handwriting, he wrote a special note. "He always made people feel good whether he knew them or not," said Greenspan. "He was my best friend."[3]

In the 1960s, African Americans had begun to push for equal rights. Sit-ins, demonstrations, clashes with police, and marches became common. In 1963, the great civil rights leader Martin Luther King, Jr., gave his famous "I Have a Dream" speech at a huge rally in Washington, D.C. Jesse Owens knew and respected Martin Luther King, Jr., especially for his speaking ability and for his genuine goodness.

Owens admired the courage of civil rights workers, but protest speeches and demonstrations made him uneasy. America had made it possible for him to rise up out of poverty, and he was grateful to the people who had helped him, both black and white. "I have always hoped to be a motivating force for good because people have given me so much," Owens once said.[4] More often a peacemaker than a fighter, he chose to suppress painful racial scars from the past. For this, some African Americans called Owens an "Uncle Tom." This was a name for blacks who cooperated with racially conservative whites instead of demanding equal rights.

In November 1963, an assassin gunned down President John F. Kennedy in Dallas, Texas. Lyndon Johnson became President. Soon after, Congress passed the federal Civil Rights Act of 1964. It banned discrimination in public places, transportation, and jobs. A later bill, the Voting Rights Act, removed restrictions that kept many African Americans in the South from voting. These actions were important first steps to improve the world in which Jesse Owens and other African Americans lived.

In 1964, Jesse Owens reflected on the racism of another era. He and Ruth returned to Berlin with Bud Greenspan and his wife, Cappy. Together they made a movie about the 1936 Olympics, called *Jesse Owens Returns to Berlin*. Woven into the film were clips of the 1936 Olympics. As Owens walked through the empty stadium talking about the past, long-forgotten images came to life.

"The sounds of the past are in the walls, the archways, and the very ground on which I stand," he said. "The stadium is its own island. . . . Here time has always stood still."[5]

While in Berlin, Owens again saw Karl Long, the son of his late German friend, Luz Long. The two had written letters over the years. On camera, Owens told Karl how Luz Long had helped him, and about their friendship. Sprawled on the grass, Jesse posed with Karl, just as he had with Luz Long in 1936. Owens said it brought back one of his warmest memories from the Olympics.

At a screening of the film in Munich, one thousand German dignitaries gave Owens a standing ovation. Owens said, "I would like to thank Cappy and Bud Greenspan for making this film. In 1936, eighty thousand people saw me run. Thirty-six years later, two hundred million people can see me run."[6] Greenspan recalled dining out with Owens the night after the film aired on television in one hundred countries. When Owens entered the restaurant, everyone stood and applauded.

In February 1965, the fledgling New York Mets baseball team asked Owens to help the players in Florida as a running coach. Owens welcomed the chance to do something physical. He still walked on his toes, as if ready to sprint down a cinder track. But shortly after he returned from Florida, he landed in the hospital. A ruptured disk in his back left him paralyzed briefly, until surgery corrected the problem.

That fall, he battled a different kind of problem. The Internal Revenue Service filed suit against him because he had not sent in the proper income tax forms for the years 1954–1962. Constantly on the go, Owens had not kept careful records and had often left his financial accounting to others. In court, Owens was found guilty as charged. He could have faced a $40,000 fine and gone to jail for four years. To his great relief, the judge set the fine at $3,000 with no jail sentence.[7] The judge said that Owens's positive national image and years of public service made up for his crime. Owens also had to pay $68,166 in back taxes. Loyal friends helped Owens pay some of that debt.

The late 1960s drew Owens and the rest of the United States into the growing civil rights movement. Owens went to the 1968 Olympics in Mexico City as a consultant for the United States Olympic Committee. African-American sprinters Tommie Smith and John Carlos came in first and third in the 200-meter race. The crowd gasped when the two athletes lowered their heads and raised black-gloved fists skyward when "The Star-Spangled Banner" was played. Their silent protest against civil rights violations back home made headlines worldwide.

After the incident, Jesse Owens tried to convince Smith and Carlos to apologize to the Olympic committee. They refused and were thrown off the United States team.

Jesse Owens sympathized with the cause of this new generation of angry African-American athletes, but his approach differed from theirs. He said, "I came back to the United States after four gold medal victories in Berlin to the same segregation that I left. I have sat in more backs of busses, been ushered into more 'Black' washrooms, and slept in more flea-bitten third-class hotels than one would want to remember." He recalled times when he had been invited to speak at hotels that would not rent him a room. He said of those who protested, "You are fighting the good battle . . . but fight it on the right battlefield. The Olympic arena is not that battlefield."[8]

When Jesse Owens returned home, he teamed with writer Paul G. Neimark and wrote two books, published in 1970. In *The Jesse Owens Story*, he said, "In America, anyone can still become somebody."[9] He told kids to be the best they could be, no matter what that was. In *Blackthink: My Life as Black Man and White Man*, he sharply criticized African Americans who blamed all their failures on prejudice. In a later book, *I Have Changed*, he softened his tone.

In 1972, when Owens was almost sixty, Ohio State gave him an honorary doctorate of athletic arts. In 1974, he was inducted into the Track and Field Hall of Fame.

He continued to inspire young people. At a 1973 track meet, he met a promising African-American sprinter and long jumper named Carl Lewis, age twelve. Owens praised the boy and told him to have fun running and jumping. Owens could not know that Lewis would go on to win a record nine gold medals in the 1984, 1988, 1992, and 1996 Olympics.

In 1976, Owens received the nation's highest peacetime civilian honor, the Presidential Medal of Freedom. President Gerald R. Ford said Owens inspired all Americans. Owens also wrote another book, called *Track and Field*. He gave tips, such as telling runners to think of their arms as "a pendulum on a clock with the swinging motion in a straight line toward the finish." Repeating Coach Riley's advice from long ago, Owens stressed determination, dedication, and discipline. He said those three traits were "a ladder you climb, not just in track but in everything you do in life."[10]

After years of frantic traveling, Jesse Owens finally retired with Ruth in 1978 to a new home in Scottsdale, Arizona. On holidays they visited their daughters and their families in Chicago. Owens was close to his five grandchildren—Donna, Gina, Dawn, Marlene,

Throughout his life, Jesse Owens was never too busy to sign autographs, especially for children. He asked the person's name, and then wrote a special note along with his autograph.

and Stuart. "He probably spent more time with the grandchildren than he had been able to spend with his own children," said Marlene Owens Rankin.[11]

That year, Owens published *Jesse: A Spiritual Autobiography*. He dedicated the book to Ruth Owens, Luz Long, his parents, Charles Riley, and to the "Great Referee [God]."[12] The text reflected Owens's deeply rooted religious beliefs and contained lines from the poem "Excelsior," given to him by Charles Riley thirty-five years before. In 1979, President Jimmy Carter awarded Owens, then sixty-six, the Living Legends award because he had inspired others to excel.

Just when his life seemed to have quieted down, Jesse Owens began to feel tired and short of breath. As a child, his lungs had been weak. A bout with pneumonia in 1971 had almost killed him. In his later years, he had smoked cigarettes and a pipe. In the fall of 1979, doctors in Chicago made the grim diagnosis—lung cancer. His wife and daughters prepared for the worst.

Jesse Owens remained the perfect gentleman to the end. Polite and kind, he dressed neatly in designer warm-up suits, even as his physical strength weakened. On March 29, 1980, Owens slipped into a coma. In two days, he was gone.

At the news of his death, flags flew at half-mast in Arizona. Two thousand people trudged through freezing cold and snow to attend his funeral in Chicago.

A silk Olympic flag, with its five intertwined rings, covered the gleaming casket. Speakers struck a positive, upbeat tone that would have pleased Jesse Owens. One quipped that Ralph Metcalfe (who had died the year before) had probably met Owens at the gates to Heaven, saying, "I beat you this time. I got here first."[13]

Jesse Owens once wrote, "The lives of most men are patchwork quilts."[14] The golden squares in Owens's patchwork quilt were his numerous track records, medals, and awards. But the other squares also held bold, bright colors—symbols of his work with young people, as an ambassador of goodwill, and as a motivational speaker.

Charles Riley had advised Jesse as a young boy to dig deep within for courage, saying that "the only victory that counts is the one over yourself."[15] In that sense, Jesse Owens never did stop running. He cleared huge hurdles—illness, poverty, and racial bigotry. Able to run and jump with a smooth, nearly perfect grace, his finely tuned body was beautiful, agile, and swift. He smashed records in an era when records were harder to set—long before streamlined tracks, starting blocks, computer-recorded finishes, and brand-name running shoes became part of track and field. In his later years, Jesse Owens continued to strive for excellence, because he believed that "life—the inner life—is the true Olympics."[16]

AFTERWORD

After Jesse Owens's death, monuments honoring him were erected in Alabama and Ohio, among other places. The citizens of Berlin, Germany, named a street leading to the Olympic stadium "Jesse Owens Allee."

Five members of the Owens family, spanning three generations, have attended Ohio State University. In Jesse Owens's honor, the school named a track in the stadium after him, and created the Jesse Owens Plaza, where a free-form bronze sculpture stands. Engraved on the walls of the monument are quotes from his many speeches.

In 1980, family and friends founded the Jesse Owens Foundation in Chicago, Illinois, to perpetuate his spirit and to encourage young people to realize their potential. Ruth S. Owens is chairman of the board. Marlene Owens Rankin is executive director. Gloria Owens Hemphill and Beverly Owens Prather also take active roles.

Two of Jesse Owens's grandchildren, Gina Hemphill Tillman and Stuart Owen Rankin, helped carry the Olympic torch on its cross-country journey to the 1996 Olympics.

CHRONOLOGY

1913—James Cleveland Owens born in Oakville, Alabama, on September 12.

1922—Owens family moves to Cleveland, Ohio; Jesse enters Bolton Elementary School.

1927 —Attends Fairmount Junior High School; meets
–1930 Charles Riley; breaks two records for junior high athletes in the high jump and the long jump; meets Minnie Ruth Solomon.

1930—Enters East Technical High; joins the track team.

1933—At the National Interscholastic Championship meet in Chicago, ties national record for high schools in the 100-yard dash, sets new world record in the 220-yard dash; enters Ohio State University.

1934—Elected by the Amateur Athletic Union to All-America Track and Field Team.

1935—At the Big Ten Track and Field Championships in Ann Arbor, ties the world record in the 100-yard dash, and sets new world records in the long jump, 220-yard sprint, and 220-yard hurdles; marries Ruth Solomon.

1936—At the Olympics in Berlin, wins four gold medals in the 100-meter and 200-meter races, the long jump, and the 400-meter relay; signs contract with agent Marty Forkins, loses his amateur status.

1937 —Works at a variety of jobs to support his wife and
–1940 three daughters—as a band leader, owner of basketball and softball teams, performer at track exhibitions, partner in a dry cleaning business.

1940—Returns to Ohio State University; works as an assistant track coach and runs a dry cleaning business.

1941—Hired by the United States Office of Civilian
–1949 Defense; becomes a personnel director for Ford Motor Company; moves to Chicago as a promotional executive for a clothing store.

1950—Named the greatest track and field athlete by the
–1960 Associated Press (AP); works with boys' clubs, Scout troops, and delinquent youths; acts as goodwill ambassador for the State Department and as one of President Eisenhower's representatives at the 1956 Olympics; forms a public relations agency; becomes a popular motivational speaker.

1960—Appears on *This Is Your Life*; makes film *Jesse*
–1978 *Owens Returns to Berlin*; attends 1968 Olympics; writes four books; receives honorary doctorate of athletic arts; inducted into the Track and Field Hall of Fame; receives the Presidential Medal of Freedom.

1978—Retires with Ruth Owens to Scottsdale, Arizona; receives Living Legend Award.

1980—Dies of lung cancer in Arizona, March 31.

CHAPTER NOTES

Chapter 1

1. Jesse Owens with Paul G. Neimark, *The Jesse Owens Story* (New York: G. P. Putnam's Sons, 1970), pp. 33, 35.

2. Barbara Moro, Interview with Jesse Owens and Ruth Owens, 1961, Illinois State Historical Library, Springfield, Illinois, tape 3, transcript p. 11.

3. Bud Greenspan, *Jesse Owens Returns to Berlin*, Cappy Productions, Inc. (Hollywood: Paramount, 1964, 1988).

4. Cleveland *Call and Post,* April 15, 1937, cited in William J. Baker, *Jesse Owens: An American Life* (New York: The Free Press, 1986), p. 94.

5. "Olympic Games," *Time*, August 17, 1936, p. 37.

Chapter 2

1. Jesse Owens with Paul Neimark, *Jesse: A Spiritual Autobiography* (Plainfield, N. J.: Logos International, 1978), p. 6.

2. Ibid., p. 9.

3. Ibid., p. 5.

4. William J. Baker, *Jesse Owens: An American Life* (New York: The Free Press, 1986), p. 7.

5. Owens with Neimark, p. 5.

6. Moro, p. 4.

7. Owens with Neimark, p. 16.

8. Baker, pp. 10–11.

9. Owens with Neimark, p. 18.

10. Ibid., p. 22.

Chapter 3

1. Barbara Moro, Interview with Jesse Owens and Ruth Owens, 1961, Illinois State Historical Library, Springfield, Illinois, tape 1, transcript p. 11.

2. Jesse Owens with Paul Neimark, *Jesse: A Spiritual Autobiography* (Plainfield, N. J.: Logos International, 1978), p. 30.

3. Moro, p. 41.

4. Ibid., p. 24

5. Jesse Owens with Paul G. Neimark, *Blackthink: My Life as Black Man and White Man* (New York: William Morrow and Company, Inc., 1970), p. 159.

6. Jesse Owens with Paul G. Neimark, *The Jesse Owens Story* (New York: G. P. Putnam's Sons, 1970), p. 32.

7. Owens with Neimark, *Jesse: A Spiritual Autobiography*, p 41.

8. Undated newspaper clipping in Ohio State University Special Collections.

9. William J. Baker, *Jesse Owens: An American Life* (New York: The Free Press, 1986), p. 24.

10. Owens with Neimark, *Jesse: A Spiritual Autobiography*, p. 37.

Chapter 4

1. Jesse Owens with Paul G. Neimark, *Blackthink: My Life as Black Man and White Man* (New York: William Morrow and Company, Inc., 1970), p. 91.

2. Jesse Owens with Paul Neimark, *Jesse: A Spiritual Autobiography* (Plainfield, N. J.: Logos International, 1978), p. 44.

3. Isi Newborn, "Owens Meets Metcalfe in Title Clash," *Cleveland Press*, June 26, 1933, p. 1.

4. *Chicago Defender*, June 10, 1933, cited in William J. Baker, *Jesse Owens: An American Life* (New York: The Free Press, 1986), p. 31.

5. Stuart Bell, "Jesse Owens a Gamester: He Has Yet to Fall Down. Why Pick on Promoters?" *Cleveland Press*, June 19, 1933.

6. Barbara Moro, Interview with Jesse Owens and Ruth Owens, 1961, Illinois State Historical Library, Springfield, Illinois, tape 2, transcript p. 10.

7. Henry Wadsworth Longfellow, "Excelsior," in *Selected Poems of Henry Wadsworth Longfellow* (New York: Random House Value Publishing, 1992), p. 678.

Chapter 5

1. Isi Newborn, "Dash Rivals Bid for New '100' Mark," *Cleveland Press*, June 30, 1933.

2. Larry Snyder, "My Boy Jesse," *Saturday Evening Post,* November 7, 1936, p. 15.

3. Jesse Owens with Paul Neimark, *Jesse: A Spiritual Autobiography* (Plainfield, N. J.: Logos International, 1978), p. 155.

4. Barbara Moro, Interview with Jesse Owens and Ruth Owens, 1961, Illinois State Historical Library, Springfield, Illinois, tape 1, transcript p. 64.

5. Snyder, p. 100.

6. Jack Clowser, "Go With Clowser to Ann Arbor and Thrill to Owens' Big Day," *The Cleveland News*, May 27, 1938.

Chapter 6

1. Barbara Moro, Interview with Jesse Owens and Ruth Owens, 1961, Illinois State Historical Library, Springfield, Illinois, tape 2, transcript p. 22.

2. Ibid., tape 1, p. 59.

3. Jesse Owens with Paul G. Niemark, *Blackthink: My Life as Black Man and White Man* (New York: William Morrow and Company, Inc., 1970), pp. 15–20.

Chapter 7

1. Jesse Owens with Paul Neimark, *Jesse: A Spiritual Autobiography* (Plainfield, N. J.: Logos International, 1978), p. 60.

2. Barbara Moro, Interview with Jesse Owens and Ruth Owens, 1961, Illinois State Historical Library, Springfield, Illinois, tape 2, transcript p. 28.

3. Jesse Owens Diary, 7/25–7/27, cited in William J. Baker, *Jesse Owens: An American Life* (New York: The Free Press, 1986), p. 83.

4. Larry Snyder, "My Boy Jesse," *Saturday Evening Post*, November 7, 1936, p. 15.

5. Bud Greenspan, *Jesse Owens Returns to Berlin*, Cappy Productions, Inc. (Hollywood: Paramount, 1964, 1988).

Chapter 8

1. Bud Greenspan, *100 Greatest Moments in Olympic History* (Los Angeles: General Publishing Group, Inc., 1995), p. 14.

2. Bud Greenspan, *Jesse Owens Returns to Berlin*, Cappy Productions, Inc. (Hollywood: Paramount, 1964, 1988).

3. William J. Baker, *Jesse Owens: An American Life* (New York: The Free Press, 1986), p. 91.

4. Greenspan, *Jesse Owens Returns to Berlin*.

5. Jesse Owens with Paul Neimark, *Jesse: A Spiritual Autobiography* (Plainfield, N. J.: Logos International, 1978), pp. 64–65.

6. Greenspan, *Jesse Owens Returns to Berlin*.

7. Grantland Rice, *The Tumult and the Shouting: My Life in Sport* (New York: Barnes, 1954), p. 252.

8. Greenspan, *100 Greatest Moments in Olympic History*, p. 19.

9. Jesse Owens and Paul G. Neimark, *The Jesse Owens Story* (New York: G. P. Putnam's Sons, 1978), p. 71.

10. Martha Dodd, *Through Embassy Eyes* (New York: Harcourt Brace, 1939), p. 212, cited in Baker, p. 100.

11. Ibid., p. 212, cited in Baker, p. 101.

12. William O. Johnson, Jr., *All That Glitters Is Not Gold* (New York: G. P. Putnam's Sons, 1972), p. 179.

13. Greenspan, *100 Greatest Moments in Olympic History*.

14. Barbara Moro, Interview with Jesse Owens and Ruth Owens, 1961, Illinois State Historical Library, Springfield, Illinois, tape 3, transcript p. 8.

15. Greenspan, *Jesse Owens Returns to Berlin*.

Chapter 9

1. Norman Katkov, "Jesse Owens, the Ebony Express," *Sport*, April 1954, p. 29.

2. Personal interview with Bud Greenspan, April 4, 1996.

3. Larry Snyder, "My Boy Jesse," *Saturday Evening Post*, November 7, 1937, p. 98.

4. Ibid., pp. 97–98.

5. Larry Snyder, "The World's Greatest Track Athlete," *Scholastic Coach*, March, 1936, pp. 30–32.

6. *Chicago Defender*, August 5, 1936, cited in William J. Baker, *Jesse Owens: An American Life* (New York: The Free Press, 1986), p. 111.

7. *The New York Times*, August 17, 1936, cited in William J. Baker, *Jesse Owens: An American Life*, p. 118.

8. William J. Baker, *Sports in the Western World* (Totowa, N.J.: Rowman and Littlefield, 1981), p. 256.

Chapter 10

1. Barbara Moro, Interview with Jesse Owens and Ruth Owens, 1961, Illinois State Historical Library, Springfield, Illinois, tape 3, transcript p. 22.

2. Bud Greenspan, *Jesse Owens Returns to Berlin*, Cappy Productions, Inc. (Hollywood: Paramount, 1964, 1988).

3. Jesse Owens with Paul G. Neimark, *Jesse: A Spiritual Autobiography* (Plainfield, N. J.: Logos International, 1978), p. 81.

4. Ibid., pp. 83–84.

5. Jesse Owens with Paul G. Neimark, *The Jesse Owens Story* (New York: G. P. Putnam's Sons, 1970), p. 36.

6. Ibid., p. 77.

7. "The Olympic Games," *Time*, August 17, 1936, p. 37.

8. William J. Baker, *Jesse Owens: An American Life* (New York: The Free Press, 1986), p. 138.

9. Ibid., pp. 139–140.

10. William O. Johnson, Jr., *All That Glitters Is Not Gold* (New York: G. P. Putnam's Sons, 1972), p. 47.

Chapter 11

1. Barbara Moro, Interview with Jesse Owens and Ruth Owens, 1961, Illinois State Historical Library, Springfield, Illinois, tape 3, transcript p. 25.

2. Jesse Owens with Paul Neimark, *Jesse: A Spiritual Autobiography* (Plainfield, N. J.: Logos International, 1978), p. 89.

3. Ibid., p. 95.

4. *Cleveland Call and Post*, August 25, 1938, and September 1, 1938, cited in William J. Baker, *Jesse Owens: An American Life* (New York: The Free Press, 1986), p. 155.

5. Owens with Neimark, p. 97.

6. Ibid., pp. 99–101.

7. Ibid., p. 123.

8. *Cleveland Call and Post*, August 27, 1936, cited in William J. Baker, *Jesse Owens: An American Life*, p. 14.

9. Owens with Neimark, pp. 118–120.

10. Ibid., p. 125.

11. E. D. Hirsch, Jr., Joseph F. Kett, and James Trefil, *The Dictionary of Cultural Literacy* (Boston: Houghton Mifflin Company, 1988), p. 276

Chapter 12

1. William O. Johnson, Jr., *All That Glitters Is Not Gold* (New York: G. P. Putnam's Sons, 1972), p. 40.

2. Bud Greenspan, *100 Greatest Moments in Olympic History* (Los Angeles: General Publishing Group, Inc., 1995), p. 13.

3. The Jesse Owens Foundation pamphlet, pp. 1, 3, 1996.

4. Jesse Owens with Paul G. Neimark, *Blackthink: My Life as Black Man and White Man* (New York: William Morrow and Company, Inc., 1970), p. 134.

5. Barbara Moro, Interview with Jesse Owens and Ruth Owens, 1961, Illinois State Historical Library, Springfield, Illinois, tape 5, transcript pp. 15, 33.

6. Personal interview with Marlene Owens Rankin, March 22, 1996.

7. Ibid.

8. Ibid.

9. Jesse Owens with Paul Neimark, *Jesse: A Spiritual Autobiography* (Plainfield, N. J.: Logos International, 1978), pp. 132–135.

10. Ibid., p. 136.

11. Undated manuscript on Jesse Owens at Illinois Historical Society, p. 2.

12. Undated press clipping from Philadelphia newspaper in Ohio State University Special Collection.

13. Personal interview with Marlene Owens Rankin, March 22, 1996.

14. Owens with Neimark, *Blackthink: My Life as Black Man and White Man*, p. 96.

15. Steven Gietschier, "The Greatest Day: Jesse Owens at Ann Arbor," *Timeline,* a publication of the Ohio Historical Society, May/June, 1994, p. 7.

Chapter 13

Chapter title: Jesse Owens, in Barbara Moro interview with Jesse Owens and Ruth Owens, 1961, Illinois State Historical Library, Springfield, Illinois, tape 4, p. 25.

1. Personal interview with Bud Greenspan, April 4, 1996.

2. Ibid.

3. Ibid.

4. The Jesse Owens Foundation pamphlet, 1996, p. 9.

5. Bud Greenspan, *Jesse Owens Returns to Berlin*, Cappy Productions, Inc. (Hollywood: Paramount, 1964, 1988).

6. Personal interview with Bud Greenspan, April 4, 1996.

7. Jesse Owens with Paul Neimark, *Jesse: A Spiritual Autobiography* (Plainfield, N. J.: Logos International, 1978), p. 200.

8. "A Conversation with Jesse Owens," undated memo in possession of Marlene Owens Rankin, March 22, 1996.

9. Jesse Owens with Paul G. Neimark, *The Jesse Owens Story* (New York: G. P. Putnam's Sons, 1970), p. 9.

10. Jesse Owens, *Track and Field*, ed. Dick O'Connor (New York: Atheneum, 1976), pp. 13–14, 116.

11. Personal interview with Marlene Owens Rankin, March 22, 1996.

12. Owens with Neimark, *Jesse: A Spiritual Autobiography*, dedication page.

13. *Chicago Tribune*, April 5, 1980, cited in William J. Baker, *Jesse Owens: An American Life* (New York: The Free Press, 1986), p. 226.

14. Jesse Owens with Paul Neimark, *I Have Changed* (New York: William Morrow and Company, Inc., 1972), p. 17.

15. Owens with Neimark, *Jesse: A Spiritual Autobiography*, p. 61.

16. Ibid., p. 45.

FURTHER READING

Baker, William J. *Jesse Owens: An American Life*. New York: The Free Press, 1986.

————. *Sports in the Western World*. Totowa, N.J.: Rowman and Littlefield, 1981.

Gietschier, Steven. "The Greatest Day: Jesse Owens at Ann Arbor." *Timeline*, a publication of the Ohio Historical Society, May/June, 1994.

Greenspan, Bud. *Jesse Owens Returns to Berlin*, Cappy Productions, Inc. Hollywood: Paramount, 1964, 1988.

————. *100 Greatest Moments in Olympic History*. Los Angeles: General Publishing Group, Inc., 1995.

Jesse Owens Foundation, 401 North Michigan Avenue, Chicago, Illinois 60611.

Owens, Jesse, with Paul G. Neimark, *The Jesse Owens Story*. New York: G. P. Putnam's Sons, 1970.

————, with Paul G. Neimark. *Blackthink: My Life as Black Man and White Man*. New York: William Morrow and Company, Inc., 1970.

————, with Paul Neimark, *Jesse: A Spiritual Autobiography*. Plainfield, N. J.: Logos International, 1978.

————, with Paul Neimark. *I Have Changed*. New York: William Morrow and Company, Inc., 1972.

————. *Track and Field*, ed. Dick O'Connor. New York: Atheneum, 1976.

Snyder, Larry. "My Boy Jesse." *Saturday Evening Post*, November 7, 1936.

INDEX

19.95